Published by Gin & Tonic Press
www.gintonicpress.com

ISBN 978-0-9887049-4-7
Ebook ISBN: 978-0-9887049-0-9

FOR GREY & TESSA

DISCLAIMER

Normally, this where you'd read:

All characters appearing in this work are fictitious. Any resemblance to real persons, living or dead, is purely coincidental.

Which, for the most part, is true. In this work, however, a little more needs to be said.

Several of the characters here are clearly named after and based on real persons, i.e., the famous ones. That said, those actual portrayals are entirely fictitious, satirical, and do not depict actual events or words spoken by those individuals. Think of them as fictional versions of those persons, capable of actions entirely inconsistent with the real individual, existing in a parallel universe along with Evil Kirk.

INTRODUCTION

The rather silly journey you're about to read, took a journey of its own. It started as a short story first written amid the financial collapse of 2008 for my own amusement, which simply grew in length, before arriving in its final resting place in 2013 as the novel you now hold. In that time many changes have occurred in the world, such as the explosion of ebooks in the form of the iPad, Kindle et al., as well as a minor uptick in the economic situation. Of course, by the time you're reading this, things might have turned to the better... or to the much, much worse. So, while I thought of updating the story, of moving it from its moment in time before the so-called *Great Recession*, I decided there was enough about it, no matter what the circumstance, which would remain relevant and that time would merely date it once more. Regardless, economies move in cycles so, wait a moment and it will be prescient once again. I wrote it mostly as an amusing diversion which, coincidentally, is also how it is intended to be read. So cast your mind back to those heady days of 2008, when it seemed as if the housing market would defy the laws of economic physics and never come down, just like the dotcom explosion before it—those days of bliss.

Enjoy.

-CJR

THE
SIEGE OF
WALTER PARKS

A NOVEL
BY COLIN ROBERTSON

GIN & TONIC PRESS
GINTONICPRESS.COM

CHAPTER 1

"It's nothing to write home about." - Odysseus

Plansville, New Jersey was an idyllic suburban community. It was more idyllic than Watersbridge, just to the South, and only slightly less so than Eldergrove, the gold standard of suburban development to the North. Eldergrove, of course, had the advantage of having been zoned to include a golf course. Plansville said that it had never wanted a golf course to begin with—that golf courses meant errant golf balls and men in ugly plaid trousers that made one's eyeballs itch. Eldergrove could keep its damn golf course, Plansville was very happy with itself and a dog park was more practical anyway.

Not that there was anything wrong with Plansville. It was exactly as advertised and advertised it had been—magazine spreads, radio commercials and even a few local television spots. The houses were attractive, the grass green, and the lots surprisingly spacious. Inside of each home was the requisite travertine tile bathrooms, kitchen with granite countertops and beautiful stainless steel dishwashers from Bosch on which no one could find the on button (and that was the point). Every lawn sprinkler in Plansville cast a sunshine rainbow promising its own private pot of gold. "Claim your kingdom!" said one of the billboards. That's what had drawn Walter Parks there, the opportunity to own his own personal plot of paradise where he too could receive brochures for roof repair. For most of the community's residents it was all perfectly natural, but for Walter it never seemed quite right.

To start with, Walter never felt like an adult. He certainly had all of the trappings of one; a faithful wife, a baby daughter, and now, a big beautiful home. Still, there were times he would stop and wonder when a man in a suit would show up on his doorstep and say, "I'm sorry, there's been some mistake, none of this really belongs to you."

Walter's house was on Dream Street. If that seems a trifle contrived, that's because it was. Every street name in Plansville had been carefully contrived by a group of marketing professionals, The Mitchell-Danforth Group, from Madison Avenue. The names had been gathered from brainstorming sessions; group tested and ran through a sieve of market research. As a result, Dream Street ran parallel to Paradise Lane, and both of them crossed Aspiration Road. The designers wanted buyers to feel as if they had found something too perfect to be real, and yet here it was, drywall and all, starting at just five hundred and ninety-nine thousand.

Walter's house was the last house on the block. His one adjacent neighbour was Stephen Prefect. It would be easy to confuse the two houses on paper as the floor plans were identical but mirrored, exactly reversed in ever detail. Everything in Plansville was regulated to maintain the community's idyllic status, which meant every house had to conform to an ideal state. Residents, for example, could only fill their gardens with plants from a list of acceptable flora. There would be no renegade rhododendrons upsetting the perennial perfection of Dream Street.

In reality, Walter's house was unmistakable. It was distinguished by the presence of an enormous billboard on his front lawn. On the billboard a smiling family hugged one another beneath a blue sky and proclaimed, "Own your own American Dream!" Walter had no idea who these people were. They were stock photography models. The man was an out-of-work actor with a drug problem, and the woman was a runway model who now, over the fatal age of thirty, had to take whatever work she could get. The little boy was an unwilling child actor and the little girl was a digital Frankenstein's creation, Photoshopped from the facial features of five different girls. With the second half of Plansville as yet unfinished, the realtors had brokered a deal with Walter. They would knock a percentage off his sale price if he agreed to leave the billboard on his front lawn for two years. The percentage had made the difference that had allowed Walter to buy in, so the decision was an easy one. As a result, his house was "the one with the billboard". Steve Prefect's house was "next to the house with the billboard", the Jennings' house was "two houses down from the one with the billboard" and so on. Walter's house was a landmark his neighbours wished would go away.

The only other distinguishing feature to each of the homes were the cars. The Jennings had an Infiniti FX-35 SUV and a Toyota Prius. Steve Prefect had two beautifully engineered Mercedes Benz E-Class Sedans in his driveway. Walter often wondered why his neighbour needed two such similar cars when Steve was single and lived alone. The Parks themselves had a single 1999 Chevrolet Cavalier. The Cavalier had, at this time, the distinction of being possibly the last truly reliable American automobile. Of course, part of that reliability included being reliably dull, and reliably unhappy on hills that went up as well as down, but also included reliably getting one from point A to point B. Not quickly and not in style, mind you, but eventually, and that was what mattered most to Walter Parks.

* * *

On this particular morning, all of the various cars were in their respective driveways. Walter Parks's wife Dawn could observe them all as she prepared scrambled eggs for three. Dawn Parks was herself, quite simply, beautiful. She had flowing blond hair, shining eyes and the sort of bright smile that instantly told you that yes, she was as kind as she was beautiful, yes, she really meant it, and yes, even though she could, she never would, judge you. Judging wasn't in Dawn's makeup. She believed that was someone else's job. Above the oven hung an embroidered tapestry depicting John the Baptist waist deep in water with arms open and the words "Cleanliness is next to Godliness" Dawn's kitchen was immaculate.

Dawn turned the eggs with a practiced hand and switched off the element. "Walter? Walter, you're going to be late for your meeting!"

"Coming!" Walter called from the bedroom.

Dawn turned with a smile to check on their baby girl, Hope, who sat perched in her highchair all pudgy arms and blond curls. Hope smiled back and blew bubbles gleefully from her tiny pink mouth. Dawn carefully wiped the dribble from her daughter's chin. Hope giggled with delight at her mother's attention, and then sneezed.

"God bless you!" smiled Dawn. Hope who had been momentarily bewildered by this explosion in her own nose, was reassured and smiled and gurgled happily once more.

As Walter himself had said many times to many different people, "Dawn and our baby girl, Hope, are the twin lights of my life. How I ended up with Dawn I'll never quite understand. It isn't just that she is pretty much perfect in every way, she was also raised a devout Baptist, while I'm not even sure if I believe in God. I've asked her, of course, why she would ever want to marry me, in spite of her family's deep disapproval. She told me that she had always been taught to hate the sin, love the sinner, and love me she does."

At that moment a lanky, unleashed elastic band of energy in the form of a grey Weimaraner dog bounded into the room, rebounded off of the kitchen cabinets and pounced onto Hope's dangling bare feet. There, the delighted dog began to enthusiastically lick the baby's toes. At the touch of that pink, slobbery tongue, Hope giggled gleefully.

Dawn's religious leanings had led to few conditions on their shared life; Hope would go to church and Sunday school when she was older and both she and the dog would have religious names. Hope, of course, was Hope, while the dog's name was... a bit more controversial.

Dawn opened the garbage to dispose of the excess bacon grease. The opening of the door alerted the dog who looked up curiously, one ear folded over its head like a bad combover. Upon spotting the stream of scrumptious liquefied lard, the dog immediately plunged headfirst into the garbage.

"Jesus! Jesus get out of there!" Dawn yanked Jesus back by the collar and closed the cupboard door. "No!"

It had never occurred to Dawn that some might find naming their dog 'Jesus' offensive. Jesus was a good dog who loved everyone unconditionally. So it was, in her view, entirely appropriate. It was Walter who felt embarrassed standing on the street corner at night calling his name.

* * *

While all of this was happening, Walter was still in the bedroom. Their bedroom was, for the most part, as immaculate as the rest of their home. This in spite of Walter's tendency to leave his socks in a variety of new and exciting places for Dawn to find. Above their bed hung a cross, while the rest of the walls were decorated with a collection of family photos. One collection was of Dawn and Walter on their wedding day, posing on the front steps of the church and under a tree on the front lawn. Dawn smiled in her usual beautiful transcendent way, while Walter beamed with the sort of stupefied grin of a man who's just discovered he's wearing solid gold underpants and hasn't a clue where they've come from, but knows they're his to keep. It had been a very small wedding. Walter had no family to speak of, and Dawn's kin had sent their "sincere regrets". Walter's best man had been Clark, a friend from college he'd reconnected with online, but who had since disappeared. Dawn's maid of honour had been her hairdresser, Susan who had consistently referred to

Walter as "Wilbur" throughout the entire event.

The next collection of photos were baby photos of Hope. It consisted of twenty photos taken from the day of her birth to just one week ago. The photos that didn't fit on the wall were crammed into her baby book placed conveniently on the dresser. The baby book was, along with the Bible, the most important book in Dawn's life. It told the ongoing story of Hope's life in words, pictures, and mementos. To the untrained eye many of the photos there would appear almost identical; Hope lying down in a onesie or Hope sitting in a highchair, but to Walter and Dawn, each one represented a critical moment of their baby's short life thus far.

The last collection of photos on the wall was the most unexpected. They detailed an aspect of Walter's life Dawn had learned to accept and even embrace. Walter had a fetish. Not the kind of fetish that makes one dress up in black leather and join underground sadomasochistic clubs such as those in the SoHo district of New York or Harvard University. In fact, Walter's obsession had nothing to do with their love life. Rather, his fetish took the form of a keen interest in medieval history. The oldest photos were of Walter and Dawn at a renaissance fair while dating. Next came photos of Walter in a knight's costume for Halloween, Walter holding a medieval mace at a collectables convention and the most recent, Walter, Dawn and Hope at the *Medieval Times Jousting Tournament*. In that photo Walter held aloft an appropriate haunch of venison, while Dawn sipped a Diet Coke and Hope looked startled by the camera flash. All three had terrible red eye. Dawn didn't share Walter's love of all things medieval, but she knew that if he could sit through a Baptist sermon once a week for her, she could certainly attend the occasional anachronistic event with him.

This brings us to Walter. Walter Parks was standing before his dresser in a business suit but, as of yet, no tie, carefully rearranging tiny figurines on the battlefield there. Despite being thirty-five Walter had the boyish look of a man in his twenties. He was neither particularly handsome, nor unattractive. At five-eleven, he was neither short, nor tall. Walter Parks was, as if by design, a perfectly average man. In high school, the girls would only agree to go out with him when nothing better had come along. In fact, until he'd met Dawn, his entire dating life had largely been arranged by default.

"Sir Gawain should be fighting the Green Knight and..." Walter looked about. "Sir Galahad? Where the heck is Sir Galahad?"

Walter carefully scanned the throng of armoured knights slashing and parrying with swords, axes, and pikes. He then looked behind the dresser, under the dresser, and under the nearby bed. There was no sign of the lilliputian-sized hero. Walter rose to his feet wondering, "Galahad? Where did you..." His thoughts stopped at the feeling of a stabbing pain in his shoeless right heel. Bending down Walter extracted a tiny one inch sword from his own foot. He examined the clear grooves of chew marks on the blade. "Jesus."

* * *

"Jesus ate Sir Galahad," Walter announced from the kitchen entryway. He was hoping for either sympathy or a solution. He received neither.

"Well, that wouldn't happen if you didn't leave those knights out all the time," Dawn suggested as she always did.

With a scowl, Walter took his seat at the breakfast table. There, he proceeded to sulk and tie his tie. Dawn laid out plates at both of their places.

"I just don't understand how he got to them. They were on top of the dresser."

Dawn smiled. Even if it had been in Dawn's nature to do so, there was no reason to admonish Walter. The loss of the toy, or 'collectable', would suffice for that. "I suppose he moves in mysterious ways," she offered and began to eat her eggs.

Walter looked at Jesus who was currently intent on licking his own crotch. "I suppose."

Minutes later, Walter was gathering his things at the front door. Dawn checked his tie, which was fine, while Walter reviewed the contents of his briefcase. Inventory and inspection complete, he turned to her with a look of real concern, "You'll let me know what the doctor says?"

Dawn nodded, "Of course, sweetheart."

"Okay. She certainly looks fine this morning."

"Yes, she does," Dawn agreed, glancing back at Hope. "It's probably nothing."

Walter smiled reassuringly. He then held her shoulders and kissed her on the cheek before turning to blow a kiss to Hope. "Goodbye sweetheart." Hope, who had been busy stuffing Cheerios up her nose, looked up with earnest surprise.

* * *

Walter opened the front door only to find Steve Prefect standing before him, hand raised in mid-knock. "Oh, good morning, Steve."

"Jesus pooped on my lawn again."

Steve was beet red. This was the colour he normally assumed when even slightly annoyed and he was more than slightly annoyed, he was livid. When he was angry a thick vein in Steve's temple would throb, and right then it was throbbing like Steve's head was trying to make a left-hand turn. Steve was a securities trader who joined the great train of cars through the Jersey Tunnel each morning on his way to Wall Street. He wore three-thousand dollar suits and two-hundred dollar ties. Walter's suit cost the same as Steve's tie. Walter's tie cost the same as Steve's lunch. Every time Walter saw Steve's vein throb he'd wonder if it was a sign of heart trouble. Dawn worried greatly for Steve's health and had told him so one day after Jesus had dug several holes in his lawn. This had done nothing to calm Steve down at the time.

"Jesus? Are you sure? We've kept him inside. Maybe it was someone else's–"

Walter's cellphone rang. He pulled it from his pocket. The caller ID read "Countricross Mortgages".

"I'm sorry Steve, I have to take this." Walter answered the phone and exited the house at the same time, delicately side stepping past his smouldering neighbour. "Hello?"

"Yes, I'm sure," Steve interjected. "You're the only ones here with a dog big enough to leave such monolithic piles of... that!"

Steve pointed accusingly at the offending excrement on his lawn.

"Mr. Parks?" said the voice on the phone.

"Speaking," replied Walter. Covering the receiver he suggested to Steve, "Maybe it was Mrs. Carling's dog?"

The representative from Countricross Mortgages continued, "Mr. Parks, this is a courtesy call because of problems with your last two mortgage payments. Your last two payments were well below the owed amount."

"Mrs. Carling's dog is a Pekinese," countered Steve. "That pile of poop is bigger than its entire body."

"But there's been some mistake," Walter explained to the man on the phone. "The amount was much more than it should have been. I left four messages."

"Are you going to clean this up or what?" Steve moved to stand between Walter and his car door. At six-foot-two inches, he towered over Walter.

"Our records show no error, Mr. Parks, perhaps you were unaware of the *balloon payment* clause in your loan agreement?"

Walter was flummoxed.

"Well?" demanded Steve. His vein throbbed pointedly at Walter, as if it might jump off and strangle him. Walter became suddenly aware that Steve's breath smelt inexplicably of fish. Kippers for breakfast, thought Walter, really?

Walter decided to address his more immediate problem. "Fine," he said.

"So we can expect your payment?" asked the Countricross representative.

"No, I mean—wait one second please." Walter put his hand over the receiver once more and addressed Steve, "Yes, I'll clean it up."

Walter glanced at his watch, seven-thirty-five. He was going to be late, and he had a meeting this morning that Mr. Jenkins had described as "critical". Mr. Jenkins had once described a meeting to discuss the proper use of staples versus paperclips as "critical" but this time he'd seemed to really mean it.

"Mr. Parks?"

Walter uncovered the phone, "Can I speak to someone about this? I was told when we got the loan that our payments wouldn't go up."

"Mr. Parks, our records clearly show that your loan agreements include an initial introductory rate, followed by a six month increase to the full amount. It was clearly explained on page seventy-six, paragraph five."

"No, no, no, that was our credit card–"

Steve glowered at him. Walter felt like a platter of prime rib under a heat lamp at a country club buffet.

"Okay! Okay! Jesus!" Walter relented.

Jesus barked from inside the house at the sound of his name.

"Not you!" Walter shouted back.

Flustered, Walter grappled for a solution. There was no time to return to the house, and Steve was clearly not going to let this go. Desperate, Walter cradled the phone against his ear and reached down to scoop up the dog poop with his bare hands.

Steve was appalled.

"Mr. Parks, this was explained in the original documents and can be verified via–"

"Listen, this isn't a good time. Can I call you back?"

Walter dropped the poop into the trash, opened his car door, and slid inside.

"Mr. Parks, we need to receive payment within three days or–"

"I'll call you back," Walter stated firmly, and hung up. He then raised his hands to the steering wheel and stopped. He could wash his hands, but getting the smell off the steering wheel might be nothing short of impossible. Walter carefully popped open his briefcase with a clean baby finger and extracted two memos on company cost savings. With a piece of paper stuck to each soiled palm, he turned the ignition, put the car into reverse and swerved out of his driveway, leaving a still stunned Steve staring after him in shock.

CHAPTER 2

"Ow!" - I. Newton

Forty minutes later, Walter made the familiar turn into the parking lot of BlankSlate Office Supplies headquarters. At the front gate, Ed, the security guard, smiled at him warmly as he approached. Ed was a large black man, whose breakfast regularly consisted of Dunkin' Donuts doughnuts and coffee.

"Good morning, Walter!" said Ed as he waved.

"Morning, Ed!" Walter said back. He raised his hand to wave, only to realize the memo was still stuck to it. Peeling off the paper, he waved properly to the puzzled guard and drove through the gate to park in spot number 17, his assigned place. Ed shrugged, took a sugar powdered bite from a jelly doughnut and returned to his book.

Walter and Ed's interactions were limited to this daily exchange, and yet Walter had long ago decided that he liked the plump security guard more than anyone else at the entire company. Of course, neither really knew the other but that, Walter decided, was the foundation of their friendly relationship. He slammed his car door and, glancing at his watch, hurried into the glass and steel office building.

Of course, had Walter actually known the truth about Ed, he would probably have fallen over sideways in shock. Ed was not, in fact, born Edward Robinson from Cheektowaga, New York, as it read on his driver's license, but Mabula Mboya from Zimbabwe, Africa. There, he had spent several years as a General for Robert Mugabe. His primary role had been as an enforcer in the dictator's program of "equalization"— taking the property of white farmers and giving it away to non-whites. He had originally believed in the program, but soon saw that the non-white recipients were largely the friends and family of Robert Mugabe who then tended to drive the farms into destitution. Execution and torturer were all well and good when it served a purpose, he felt, but by then Mabula's heart was simply no longer in it. One day, standing over a mass grave he and his men had just spent the day filling, he gazed at the setting sun and decided that he needed to make a change. He had just finished reading *Eat, Pray, Love* and knew that he really needed to do was to find himself. He then decided that the richest country on Earth was as good a place as any to start looking.

* * *

Walter pushed open the doors to the BlankSlate lobby. With a smile and nod to the receptionist, Julie, he headed directly towards the men's room door. He had only one objective; to wash the foul smell from his hands. Walter put his hand on the bathroom door handle and turned.

"Walter!"

Walter looked back over his shoulder to see David Jenkins, President of BlankSlate Office Supplies, beaming at him with open arms. Beside Mr. Jenkins stood a stout middle aged man with a brush cut of sandy blond hair. Walter did not know who he was, but the man appeared to be sizing him up for either a suit or a coffin. Walter reluctantly let go of the Men's Room door handle.

"Mr. Jenkins, sir."

"Walter, how many times have I told you to call me 'Dave'?" Mr. Jenkins smiled nervously. "We're all family here."

"Um, sorry, sir — Dave."

Mr. Jenkins turned to his heavyset companion and explained, "Walter here is our office manager. Keeps the place running like clockwork. He's always here at eight a.m. sharp!"

"Yes... Dave," Walter confirmed. Instinctively his eyes wandered to the wall clock hanging above Julie's head. The clock had stopped at four o'clock over a week ago. No one else seemed to have noticed. Not wanting anyone to follow his gaze, Walter snapped his attention back to the conversation at hand.

"Like clockwork, eh?" said the man with a heavy German accent.

"Yes, sir. Absolutely. Like a clock that... works."

Walter smiled stupidly for an awkward moment.

"Herr Schmidt, here–" Mr. Jenkins began.

"Please, *Wilhelm*," the German interjected, warmly.

"Right, of course. Wilhelm here is interested in becoming a very good friend of the company, a very good and *important* friend." Mr. Jenkins took care to emphasize the word "important" pointedly to Walter. It was only then that Walter realized that Herr Schmidt was the reason for the "critical" meeting that morning.

"Nice to meet you." Herr Schmidt offered his hand with a warm smile.

Walter, suddenly conscious again of his own odorous hands, stared at the German's as if it were a leper's hook.

After a moment's pause, Mr. Jenkins jumped in, "Well, don't leave the man hanging there, Walter."

"Oh right, sorry."

Seeing no other option, Walter forced a smile and lightly took Schmidt's hand, hoping a soft grasp would prevent transmission of any putridness.

"I don't bite. We shake hands in Germany too, you know," Schmidt chuckled and clasped Walter's hand with an iron grip that made him wince.

"Of course," said Walter, not quite sure if he still had five fingers. "So... I'll see you in the meeting, uh, Wilhelm."

"Excellent. I am looking forward to it."

Schmidt finally released Walter from his grip, who then nodded once more and escaped into the Men's Room.

Mr. Jenkins smiled with satisfaction, "He's a good man, Walter. Knows everything that goes on here."

"He shakes hands like a girl," Schmidt observed with a scowl. The German stroked his chin thoughtfully. He wondered how it was America had ever managed to become the most powerful country on Earth. Next he wondered why it was that suddenly everything smelled like dog poop.

*   *   *

Walter huddled in the relative safety of his cubical. BlankSlate was an "open concept" office and so everyone, except Mr. Jenkins and the company Vice President, Sam Timmins, had cubicles. Mr. Jenkins always liked to stress that he had an "open door" policy and, for the most part, that was true. Most of the time his door was wide open and any employee with a problem could simply knock on the frame to be welcomed in for a friendly conversation. Lately, however, Dave's door had been closed and his assistant, Kate, had been asking people to schedule their meetings. Something was up, but no one knew for certain what it was. Sales had been slow lately, but BlankSlate had never in its history laid off a single employee.

At this moment, however, Walter's concentration was on the phone call he was trying to fit in before the meeting. He sat surrounded by the various medieval knick-knacks he had brought in to make the space his own. Each of the employees had done the same to distract from the office's orange and green carpet and gold arabesque wallpaper which, together, had been described as a look from the late epileptic period. A medieval wall calendar entitled *Castles of Europe*, currently showing the ramparts of a castle in Ireland, hung from Walter's cubicle wall. A row of Crusaders led by a four-inch tall Richard the Lion Heart charged across the top of his computer monitor. Finally, a Welsh Dragon mouse pad and bobblehead Oliver Cromwell completed his desktop collection.

"Thank you for calling Countricross Home Loans. Para español, pulse uno," said a recorded woman's voice.

A meeting alert chimed up on his computer screen. Walter clicked "OK" with the mouse. He had five minutes.

"Please listen carefully as our menu options have changed. For Countricross locations near you, press–"

Walter, having neither time nor patience for the usual labyrinth of phone menu options, pressed the zero key in the hope of connecting to a live operator.

"I'm sorry that number is not recognized. Please listen carefully as our menu options have changed."

Walter swore under his breath and glanced at his watch. It was one of *those* menus, the kind that don't let you talk to an operator. The kind whose creators properly belong on one of the lower rings of Hell. One of the fiery rings, thought Walter, as justice for having sentenced so many of their customers to the first.

The recorded voice cheerfully continued, "For Countricross Locations near you, press one. For a complete list of our available services, press two. For our website address, press three. For questions regarding–"

"Hey Walter!"

Walter glanced up to see his coworker, Donnie, leaning over his cubical wall. "What? What is it?"

"You coming to the meeting or what?" Donnie asked as he picked up one of Walter's knights and began walking him across the divider top. Donnie always did this.

Walter, in turn, did what he always did and snatched the figurine away. "I'll be there in a minute."

"You know they say the Germans might be buying us up."

"What? Who said–" Walter suddenly remembered the recorded voice droning in his ear. "Never mind. I'll be there."

He waved Donnie off and snapped his attention back to the phone call.

"... to speak to a customer service representative."

"What? Press what to speak to a customer service representative?" pleaded Walter. He pressed the zero key in frustration.

"I'm sorry that number is not recognized. Please listen carefully as our–"

Walter pressed another key.

"I'm sorry–"

And another...

"I'm–"

Walter slammed down the receiver and glared at the phone as an offending object. He then took a deep breath, straightened his tie, and headed to Conference Room "Willow".

* * *

Mr. Jenkins stood before a projected Powerpoint slide admiring his own work. The slide showed a smiling cartoon pen dancing happily around a pie chart. Mr. Jenkins believed in making his slides "entertaining". He believed this would entice his employees to pay attention to them and enjoy their work more. In a previous career, Dave Jenkins had been a baby photographer where he had made the babies look at the camera and smile with various noisemakers and toys. Above all, he believed in applying lessons learned.

Around the conference room table were Walter, Donnie, Bob from sales, Andrea from accounting, Kate, whose job it was to take minutes, and finally the guest of honour Wilhelm Schmidt. Sam Timmins was supposed to be there, of course, but hadn't been at work for days. So long as Mr. Jenkins didn't ask why, nobody else would either. There was a running joke around the office that Mr. Timmins, who was frequently gone for days at a time, had a secret life elsewhere complete with wife and family. Nobody believed this, of course, no sensible person would.

Mr. Jenkins pointed to a tiny slice of the pie, their marketshare. "Now, I know one percent seems small, however, if you look at the overall market for fine tip pens, I believe our customers have been holding off on their ink tool based expenditures and we expect a surge in sales. What I call 'pen-ed up demand'."

Mr. Jenkins looked at Schmidt and smiled expectantly. Schmidt looked back it him blankly.

"It's a joke," explained Mr. Jenkins. "Pen-ed up?"

"Pent up, ja?"

"No, no, what I'm saying is," Mr. Jenkins decided to abandon the joke, "what I'm saying is, our pens could literally explode next quarter."

"Your pens could explode?"

"Well, no..."

"Not literally," said Bob, helpfully.

"Right, not literally. When I said literally, I meant, not literally."

"Figuratively," added Bob.

"Exactly," agreed Mr. Jenkins.

Schmidt nodded, "I get it. It's a joke,"

"Right. Yes."

"Sometimes my English is not one hundred percent."

Donnie leaned over to Walter and muttered, "Sometime either is Dave's."

"What was that Donnie?" Mr. Jenkins demanded.

"Nothing. Pen-ed up demand. Funny."

Mr. Jenkins scowled at Donnie as if trying to decide how he could be blamed for the current discomfort in the room.

Schmidt smiled blissfully and they all relaxed. As long as Schmidt was happy, apparently so were they.

Walter's cellphone ringtone sounded, playing the first few chords of "It Must Be Love" by Madness. Walter silenced the ringer and glanced at the caller ID. The room stared at him expectantly.

"I'm sorry, this is my wife. We have a sick baby; this will just take a second."

"Of course, Walter, family first," smiled Mr. Jenkins.

Walter nodded gratefully and, squeezing past Donnie, exited the conference room.

As the door closed behind him, he heard Schmidt add, "Ja, we all have our priorities."

* * *

In the hallway Walter answered the call, "Hey, honey, how's our baby girl?"

Through the glass window, Walter could see the meeting continue without him. The glass grew opaque, however, as Dawn's words sank in. "What do you mean, 'a hole in her heart'? I don't understand, how can someone have hole in their heart?"

Dawn explained as best as she could.

"How can they...?" Walter tried to interject. "Okay, but..."

She was rambling. Usually, even in times of great stress, Dawn could be counted on to remain rational. Finally, Walter forced himself in, "Dawn, sweetheart, listen... listen... listen to me, please. It's going to be okay. If the doctor says it can be treated then it can be treated, right?"

Dawn agreed weakly.

"Right. Okay, so just stay calm. You, me, her, we're all going to get through this. I promise you."

Dawn said okay and asked him to come home.

"Yes, I..." Walter trailed off as he watched through the glass to where the others were talking in serious tones. "I'll be there as quickly as I can. Love you, and Hope."

Walter hung up. Behind the glass Bob said something and they all burst out laughing. Whatever the joke, it was so funny Schmidt was left wiping tears from his chubby cheeks and clapping Bob warmly on the back.

* * *

Walter drove home in daze. The emotional implosion from the call had left his brain addled and incapable of coherent thought. He sat at an intersection behind a truck with a cartoon termite chomping on a beam and saying "Don't be eaten out of house and home!" Walter numbly wondered how the termite was able to talk with its mouth full.

"A hole in her heart" made no sense to Walter. Surely people couldn't live with a hole in their heart, and yet here his daughter had apparently been living with one since birth. How could this happen?

The Siege of Walter Parks

What had gone wrong?

* * *

"Hey there, precious one," Walter whispered as he leaned over Hope's crib. Hope's feather lash eyes were closed and her tiny chest rose and fell in the gentle rhythm of sleep. Beside him, Dawn was fraught with concern, nervously moving her weight from foot to foot. Not wanting to disturb her daughter's rest, she instead clutched Hope's baby book tightly to her breast. Her eyes were red with tears. "She looks fine. She looks perfectly fine," Dawn tried to reassure herself.

Walter nodded, "What did the doctor say about the procedure?"

"He said it's expensive but that our insurance, of course, would cover it."

Walter nodded once more.

"He said, they've done it a lot and that it usually goes smoothly."

Walter nodded a third time. Nothing made sense right now, so all he could do was agree. He knew his role was to support Dawn. He wanted desperately to do so, but inside he was melting.

"He said 'usually', Walter, what does that mean?" Dawn demanded.

"It means she's going to be fine."

Dawn looked into Walter's eyes. He forced himself to look confident. Together they were an emotional house of cards, each supporting the other.

Dawn opened Hope's baby book. Slowly she turned through the large cardstock pages past Hope's baby footprint, a lock of white blond hair, ultrasounds from the pregnancy and dozens of photos since birth. "We haven't finished her baby book." Dawn turned to a yet untouched page, "Baby's First Birthday". Dawn looked at Walter and demanded, "I need to know we're going to finish her book, Walter."

Walter swallowed, the sides of his mouth twitched, "We're going to finish her book, Dawn. I swear to you, we will finish her book. You understand?"

Dawn nodded and fell into his arms. "I know you don't believe like I do Walter, but you need to pray for her. For me and for her, promise me you'll pray."

"Of course I will." Walter clutched her tightly and together they began to cry.

Jesus, sensing their distress, nuzzled his cold nose as best he could between them.

* * *

Later that night Walter sat in his home office in his pajamas, robe and socks, staring at a Google results page of information about babies born with holes in their hearts. It turned out to be quite common. The internet, however, is an encyclopedia of information written by a random collection of experts and imbeciles. While the statistics were hopeful, the stories were often horrifying. Walter felt like an imbecile himself after straining his eyes on the endless pages of information. He was now in possession of various terms he didn't really understand and explanations he didn't trust. More to the point, he felt no better than when he'd started. He felt as if the hole was in his own heart.

Deciding to make one last of go of it before resigning to bed, Walter picked up the phone and dialed.

"Thank you for calling Countricross Home Loans, our offices are now closed. Please call back during regular business hours. Monday to–"

Walter hung up the phone and switched off the light.

CHAPTER 3

"You are what you eat" (cannibal aphorism)

Somewhere in the middle of the night, Walter had decided that the best thing he could do for both Dawn and Hope was to act as nonchalantly as possible. His theory was that if he acted normally, then Dawn would act normally, Hope would sense that normality and everything would turn out normal.

Apparently, Dawn had hatched a similar plan. She forced a smile and spoke in falsetto cheery tones. Of course, her tear red eyes and shaking hands belied her own attempts at normality. When Walter accidentally poured his coffee into his cereal, Dawn simply smiled and offered to dump it for him.

Finally, Walter hugged and kissed her goodbye and headed out to his car. Steve was standing proudly beside a brand new Porsche Cayman S in the adjacent driveway. Steve had been waiting for fifteen minutes just for this moment, pretending to pick lint from the spotless hood. The whole point, after all, of owning a Porsche Cayman S was to elicit envious comments from one's friends and colleagues. Steve's colleagues, also being Wall Street Investment Bankers, already owned similar or better cars, so Walter was his best target.

"Morning Walter," said Steve.

"Good Morning Steve," Walter replied.

Walter opened the door of his Chevy and tossed in his briefcase.

Steve shook his head at his neighbour's complete failure to cooperate, "You're not going to say anything about my new car?"

"Oh, I hadn't noticed," Walter lied.

Steve scowled with annoyance. This wasn't playing out as he'd imagined it at all. "It's a Porsche Cayman S. Fast as shit," he explained.

"Really? Doesn't shit mostly just lie there?"

"Um..." It was a hard point to argue.

"No, I'm kidding, it looks very fast."

Steve smiled with relief, "Just something I thought I'd treat myself with. We're expecting big, big bonuses at the firm this quarter. We have had a stellar year. Serious returns. 2008 has been very good to us."

Walter rolled his eyes. "Apparently. Plus the Mercedes was what, six, seven months old? It was time for a change."

Steve ignored Walter's pointed remark and continued with his original script, "Of course, this is only the beginning. Once my bonus actually arrives, it may be time for me to sell this shack and get a real house."

"Right."

At this Steve actually broke into song, specifically the theme from the TV show, *The Jeffersons*. "Movin'on up, movin'on up, to the east side, to a deluxe..."

Walter stared at Steve in complete bewilderment as if trying to understand how a donkey had gained the power of human speech.

Steve stopped singing and turned to Walter with apparent concern, "You know, I could do you a serious favour — get you in on one of our special funds."

"Really?" responded Walter. Walter knew of the reserved funds created by the banks for the benefits of their own senior staff and most affluent investors. It was one of the many ways of ensuring that the rich would continue to get richer.

"Sure," Steve continued, "It's pretty exclusive, you know, for the big boys, but for you I could lower the minimum investment to say... a hundred k?"

Walter felt like a fool. "Excellent, right, well I'll get back to you on that."

"Sure thing and..." at this point Steve actually winked and fired off an imaginary pistol, "you're welcome."

* * *

A few minutes later, Walter was sitting in the slow moving procession of rush hour traffic. He had recently lost his earpiece, so he was forced to hold the cellphone to his ear as he drove, watching carefully for any police officers actually interested in enforcing the hands free law.

"...and press eight to speak with a customer service representative," the Countricross voice message concluded. Walter sighed with relief and pressed the eight key.

"Before connecting you to a customer service representative, please speak or enter your twelve digit account number, now."

Walter stared at the phone in abject horror, "What?" Realizing the futility of his objection, he then scrambled to action, cradling the phone against his ear and unlatching the briefcase on the passenger seat. He began to rifle furiously through the papers with one hand in a desperate search for the number.

"I'm sorry, I didn't recognize that account number. Please try again. Speak or enter your twelve digit account number, now."

Walter found the appropriate form and pulled it out triumphantly, just in time to see the fast approaching bumper of the car in front of him. He slammed on the brakes, sending his briefcase to the floor and its contents everywhere.

His own bumper fell an inch short of the car head, kissing the air an inch between, before rocking backwards. Walter, still clutching the form, exchanged glances with the car's driver in his rearview mirror. The man eyed Walter suspiciously.

"Damn," breathed Walter. The light at the intersection was still red, so Walter flattened out the now-crumpled sheet on the seat beside him and began urgently keying in the number, 55716...

A car honked loudly behind him. The light was now green. Cradling the phone once more, Walter slipped the car into drive.

"I'm sorry, I didn't recognize that account number."

"That's because you didn't let me finish you stupid–"

The Countricross recording didn't care what Walter thought and continued, "Please try again. Speak or enter your twelve digit account number, now."

Unable to drive and press the keys at the same time, Walter decided to try the voice recognition option. "Five, five, seven, one, six, three, one, one, zero, four, five, eight," he said in clear dulcet tones, as if reading to a child.

The Countricross Recording confirmed what it had understood in its usual patched together inflection, "Was that, five, five, seven, one, six, three, one, one, zero, five, five, eight?"

Every number was correct, Walter realized, except the third last. He wondered if he'd inhaled to hard when starting to speak. "No, four, five, eight," Walter emphasized the correction, hoping to reason with it.

"If that number is correct, press one, if not, please press two to reenter." Apparently, the recording was not interested in his explanation.

Walter thought about throwing his phone out the window. Instead, he took a deep breath and pressed the two key.

"You have indicated the number was incorrect. Speak or enter your twelve digit account number, now."

Walter noticed that the recording seemed more cheerful when saying this, as if mocking him. He exited the freeway, breathed in away from the receiver and began annunciating each syllable as if talking to a complete imbecile, "Five, five, seven, one, six, three, one, one, zero, four, five, eight."

The Countricross recording incorrectly responded, "Was that, four, four, seven, one, six, three, one, one, seven, four, five, eight?"

"No!" Walter shrieked, "It was..."

Walter stopped talking as he turned into the BlankSlate parking lot entrance. He did not want Ed thinking he was a complete lunatic.

The Countricross Recording continued into his ear, "You appear to be having trouble. To speak with an operator, say, 'Operator' or 'Main Menu' to return to the main Menu."

Ed smiled, put down his doughnut, and shouted, "Walter, m'main man!"

"You have requested 'Main Menu'. Please listen carefully as our menu options have changed. For Countricross Locations near you press–"

Walter felt as he'd been stung by a cattle prod.

"You okay, Walter?" asked Ed, seeing the stunned look on Walter's face.

Walter calmly closed his cellphone and put it into his pocket, "I'm fine, Ed. Thank you for asking."

*   *   *

Donnie approached Walter's cubicle with a look of purpose and concern. Walter was on the phone, again.

Donnie wanted to help his friend and, when Walter merely waved him off, Donnie interrupted, "Walter, I think–"

Walter silenced him with the firm stop signal.

"Walter, it's import–" Donnie tried again, but was silenced once more with a harsh stare.

"Fine," Donnie relented, shrugged, and walked away, "Whatever."

Walter, refusing to let anything distract him from the call, pressed the appropriate key.

"Before connecting you to a customer service representative," the recording continued, "please speak or enter your twelve digit account number, now."

With the care of a neurosurgeon, Walter punched each key firmly and precisely.

There was an ominous pause. Walter wondered if he was supposed to press the pound key. Some systems said to do so, while others did not. It was a fixed number of numbers, so why require it?

As if accepting defeat, the recording responded, "Thank you, now connecting you to a customer service representative."

Walter punched the air in triumph, "O frabjous day" he thought and chortled in his joy. He had defeated the voice recording Jabberwock, what could possibly go wrong now?

A phone rang on the other end and the unmistakable sound of a live human being answered, "Thank you for calling Countricross Home Loans, can I please have your twelve digit account number?"

Walter found himself mouthing silent words, then babbled, "But I just keyed in my number..."

"That information is not available to me, sir," said the Countricross Representative in a practiced tone, "Can I please have your twelve digit account number?"

"Fine," Walter calmed himself. He was through; this part was easy. He recited the number from memory.

"Thank you sir, I'm bringing up your account now. Is this Mr. Walter Parks?"

"Yes."

"Can you verify for me your street address and mother's maiden name?"

"415 Dream Street and my mother's maiden name is Igraine."

Walter waved at Mr. Jenkin's assistant, Kate. She did not return the wave. Instead, she responded only with a sad smile. Kate was always cheerful. I'll have to check in with her later, he thought, and make sure she's all right.

"Thank you, Mr. Parks, what can I do for you today?" the Countricross Representative continued.

"My last two mortgage bills were higher than they should have been," Walter explained. "I tried to call to sort this out, but then I received a call from you guys that—"

"Mr. Parks?"

"Yes?" said Walter.

"I'm sorry to interrupt, but we're no longer responsible for your account."

"You're no longer responsible? What does that mean?"

"Your mortgage was sold as part of a set of bundled securities to the Wang Hui Tau Bank of Hong Kong. So technically..."

"My mortgage was sold?" Walter didn't understand how something as large as a mortgage, which was so central to his life, could simply change hands like that. He was even more surprised to discover that he had not been consulted, or even informed until after the fact.

"Yes, sir, so you'll need to talk to them."

"To the... wait, hold on," Walter reached for a pen. "Sorry, the Wang-what bank?"

Mr. Jenkins appeared at Walter's office door. He had a peculiar look on his face. It was exactly the look a Buddhist monk might have if tasked with swatting a fly. "Walter, can you come into my office, please?"

"Wang Hui Tau," said the Countricross customer service representative.

Walter held up his finger to Mr. Jenkins to indicate he wanted one minute. "Can you spell that?"

"Walter?" said Walter's boss to the fly.

"'W'as in 'What', 'A'as in 'A', 'N'as in "Nut'..."

"Now, Walter."

Walter scribbled his best guess at the spelling and said, "Sorry, I'll have to call you back."

"I would advise you to do so sir," said the voice on the phone, "Your file shows that foreclosure proceedings have been initiated on this account."

"Foreclosure proceedings?" asked Walter. "What? How?"

"Mr. Parks, you need to pay the full amount owed on your mortgage."

Walter gestured wildly with his hands before realizing this was ineffectual on a phone call. "Okay, I understand that, and I have the money, but there's been a mistake. I paid the correct amount. Do you understand?"

"You'll need to speak with the Wang Hui Tau bank about that, sir," said the representative unhelpfully. The representative had already mentally hung up on Walter and was now playing Minesweeper on his computer. Since Walter was no longer a customer, his performance would not be evaluated on this call.

"But..."

"I really can't help you, sir."

* * *

Walter sat in Mr. Jenkins's office staring at the photos on the walls. He had studied all the photos many times before, but since the alternative items to study were Mr. Jenkins's desk, a stapler, a computer, and Mr. Jenkins himself, the photos seemed like the best option.

The photos were of various office activities, including holiday parties, birthday parties, the softball team and a team-building retreat at Yellowstone National Park. Walter himself was in almost all the photos, including the ill-fated team-building exercise. They had actually lost two members that day. Not permanently, of course, they'd simply been left behind when the group boarded the bus to head back to the hotel. Two hours later, when dead silence had greeted a sing-a-long request of "now, let's hear it from the accounting department!", the bus was turned around and the stranded employees rescued. Still, the mistake had somewhat undermined the original notion of the trip. The photo, however, taken in front of Old Faithful, was a good one. It was of the entire team, including Walter, and a bewildered older gentlemen out on an excursion from a nearby retirement home.

Mr. Jenkins was averting his eyes. Walter, eager to get back to his phone call, impatiently wondered why his boss had insisted on his presence, only to avoid speaking with him now that he was here. Walter decided to initiate the conversation. "Listen, I'm sorry about the phone call yesterday. I wouldn't have taken a personal call like that unless it was vitally important."

"Walter, I don't care about the phone call," said Mr. Jenkins grimly.

"Oh. Oh, well, great. But it was important, just so you know."

Mr. Jenkins nodded and lifted his coffee cup to his lips.

Walter decided to keep the conversation going, rather than risk it slipping back into silence, "Plus there's some crazy confusion about my house, they suddenly think..." At that moment, Walter noticed the slight tremor in Mr. Jenkins's hand. Mr. Jenkins's hands were normally steady so, Walter noted, this was either the first symptoms of a possibly terrible disease, or, Mr. Jenkins was genuinely nervous about something. Walter changed course, "I'm sorry, what did you want to see me about?"

Mr. Jenkins inhaled and nodded vigorously, although Walter had not asked a yes or no question. "Walter, you know this business; you have to expand to survive."

"Grow big or go home, as you always say." Walter agreed. The out-of-context nodding lent credence to the terrible disease theory, but nervousness still seemed more likely.

"Right. Exactly," said Mr. Jenkins with a joyless smile. "So, this is why we were very interested when the Uber Deutchland Corporation showed real interest in us."

"Of course," said Walter.

"And, now it seems that they would like to buy us up."

This, Walter decided, could only be good news. They had wanted to be bought up for some time. It explained the presence of the Germans and Mr. Jenkins's current unsettled state. Mr. Jenkins, Walter decided, was simply excited about an impending deal. Walter could, at moments such as this, be incredibly dense.

"Great! That's fantastic news! That's..." Walter trailed off. Mr

Jenkins's expression was dour. Nothing like the face one normally associates with good news. "This is fantastic news for us, isn't it?"

"Yes, for *us*, it is," Mr Jenkins agreed. Walter thought it was odd the way he had emphasized the word 'us'. Mr. Jenkin's continued, "But you know how it is with mergers. There are always a few... inevitable redundancies."

"Redundancies? I... I don't understand."

Mr. Jenkins leaned forward with earnest regret and said, "Walter, the Germans are insisting that we let you go."

"Me?" said Walter. This didn't sound like fantastic news at all. Walter was in shock, and his shocked brain was now formulating thoughts like a mastodon stuck in the Le Brea Tar Pits. This, his stunned brain reasoned, explained the previous odd inflection on the word 'us'. "Me?" he repeated numbly, "Who else?"

"Just you," said Mr. Jenkins. He then added, "But it's not personal; it's strictly a business decision."

"It's not personal?" said Walter incredulously, "It's not? I'm the only person being let go, and you're telling me, it's not personal?"

"Absolutely."

"But you constantly tell us that everyone who works here is an 'individual'."

"Absolutely. No doubt. Yes. Everyone who works here is an individual but, since you're *not* working here anymore, well... you're not." Mr. Jenkins wasn't sure that had come out quite in the comforting way he'd intended. In fact, in spite of having carefully rehearsed this conversation several times in his head, none of it was going as smoothly as he'd planned. He decided it was time to move on from the "breaking the news" part of the conversation, to the "positive outlook" part. Mr. Jenkins smiled and suggested, "You know, there are plenty of other opportunities out there."

"I don't want other opportunities."

"Oh."

Mr. Jenkins ran over the rest of his rehearsed conversation. All of it had pretty much depended on Walter wanting other opportunities. In the end of the conversation Walter was supposed to stand up, inspired by his new found freedom and thank Mr. Jenkins for setting him on the road to a bright future. Walter did not appear to be even remotely inspired. Unsure how to continue, Mr. Jenkins tapped the intercom buzzer and said, "I'm sorry, Walter. Security will show you out."

* * *

Twenty minutes later, Walter was exiting the building accompanied by Ed, the security guard. Nobody thought Ed's presence was necessary. Mr. Jenkins had explained that it was simply company policy and nothing personal. Since no one had ever been laid-off from BlankSlate before, however, Walter suspected Mr. Jenkins had made up this company policy on the spot. It didn't matter, he decided, if anyone were going to have to see him out, he was happy it was Ed.

"Sorry man, life just sucks, you know?" said Ed. This was the same thing Ed used to say to prisoners before telling the firing squad to shoot.

Walter nodded. He was carrying a box full of knick-knacks from his desk. Ed was helpfully carrying Walter's briefcase.

"Well, at least they said it wasn't personal," Ed added. This was also usually true for the prisoners. Ed rarely knew their names.

"Yes." Walter noticed the unmistakable large form of Wilhelm Schmidt heading towards the building doors from another direction. For a moment the two men exchanged cold glances. Ed and Schmidt also exchanged glances with surprised recognition and narrowing eyes. Both men had met somewhere before, in a previous life. Schmidt hurried on inside.

"I blame the foreigners," said Ed, in his best upstate New York accent. Ed would always say things like this to throw off any suspicion of his African roots. "It's not our fault. They take our jobs, they take our companies, all from right under our noses. The only thing they can't take is our dignity, right?"

They reached Walter's car. Walter slid into the front seat, placing the box in the passenger seat. He took his briefcase from Ed and tossed it in back. Walter took his Sir Oliver Cromwell bobblehead and placed it on the dash.

Ed leaned into the driver's side window and looked at Walter sympathetically. "Sometimes you just want to say enough is enough. You know what I mean?"

Walter nodded, "Yes. Thank you, Ed."

"You gonna be okay, man?"

"Sure."

"Good. I'll be prayin' for you, Walter."

Ed stood up as Walter backed out of his parking spot for the last time. Walter then gunned out onto the street, sending Oliver Cromwell flying. His task completed, Ed headed to his customary perch inside the parking booth, pondering what, if anything, could be done about Robert Mugabe.

Walter turned the corner, out of sight from the BlankSlate windows and other cars. There, he lowered his head onto the steering wheel and began to cry.

CHAPTER 4

"How low can you go?" - D. Alighieri

Saint Benedict's hospital had been founded in 1849 in what had been an old New Jersey horse barn. Founded by Jesuits and named for the eighth-century monk, the hospital, as its namesake would have wanted, was a well-ordered institution focused on healing. While subsequent staff had dropped the practices of celibacy, exchanged their black robes for white coats and actually spoke with their patients once in a while, this culture of discipline had continued. The result was a modern, efficient hospital with a high overall success rate in patient treatment. This had made it an attractive target for takeover when the New Jersey government decided to privatize the institution in 1982. Telmet Healthcare won the bidding and immediately brought in a team of efficiency experts to even further streamline the institution's operations. Careful cost-cutting had turned Saint Benedict's into the most profitable hospital in Telmet's not inconsiderable collection. It was, according to Telmet's CEO, Doug Harsby, the model of what a hospital should be. Harsby himself was later forced to step down after allegations arose that St. Benedict's had been performing unnecessary heart surgery as a means to boost profits. Since that unfortunate incident, however, St. Benedict's continued to win accolades as a premiere treatment centre.

Dawn cradled Hope in her arms as she paced nervously in the hospital hallway. She looked over anxiously at Walter.

"It's going to be okay," he assured her.

"I know," said Dawn, as she leaned over to kiss Hope's forehead. "The Lord is watching over her."

"Yes," said Walter.

Walter watched as Dawn continued to pace. The hospital was surprisingly quiet. Even the nurses' station was deserted. The only sound came from a television hanging on the wall playing CNN. Walter watched the screen as a survivor from the 2004 Asian Tsunami recounted the tale of her survival. She recalled as she and her friends, neighbours, and neighbours' children were swept away with the receding ocean. She herself had survived only by chance, thrown against a Kentucky Fried Chicken billboard caught between two lampposts. She thanked God for saving her. He put that sign there, she said, it was a sign from God.

"Mr. Parks?" said a woman's voice. Walter turned to see a Nurse. "Mr. Parks, may I speak to you for a moment?"

"Can it wait? They're about to take her away from us."

"I understand," she said, "but it's about your health insurance."

Walter blanched. Between the shock of losing his job and Hope's surgery, he hadn't thought about what unemployment might do to his health coverage. He glanced at Dawn, who was completely focused on Hope's tiny being, and had heard nothing. The nurse continued, "The insurance company says you and your family are no longer covered by them."

"I lost my job the other day," Walter explained.

The Nurse nodded sympathetically. "Does your wife have her own insurance?"

"No, and she doesn't know. With Hope's issues, I didn't want to worry her."

"I see. Mr. Parks, we can't perform this operation without either insurance or a cash payment in advance."

Walter stared at her. The nurse's countenance was cold, unmoving stone. In reality, it wasn't that the Nurse was cold or unsympathetic, but she had seen this situation many times before and knew how it played out. There was no one she could talk to, nor any other alternatives. It was better to shut down any appeals now, save the time and deal with the reality of the situation.

"Okay," said Walter as he pulled out his cheque book, "How much do you need?"

Dawn continued to rock Hope gently in her arms. She gazed down at her daughter's face in wonder that the Lord could create something so beautiful. "You're going to be feeling so much better, sweetie," she cooed, "yes, you are." Hope gurgled happily at the sound of her mother's voice.

An OR nurse quietly rolled a baby gurney down the hall towards them. "Mrs. Parks?" she said. "It's time."

Dawn nodded and kissed Hope once more on the forehead before handing her over to the nurse, who then placed her onto the gurney. For a moment Dawn thought the baby might cry but, lying there, Hope became distracted by the ceiling lights. She gazed at the florescent bulbs with the same uncomprehending wonder as primitive men once gazed at the stars. Lost in her heavenly musings, Hope contemplatively sucked on all four fingers of her right hand. It was, she'd decided sometime ago, the tastier of her two hands.

Walter raced over anxiously. "Don't you dare leave without saying goodbye, pumpkin," he said as he leaned over to kiss her. "Little pumpkin," he repeated. He began to make gentle chirping noises, overcome with the sort of desperate love for his daughter that reduces adult men to blithering idiots. Hope only encouraged this behaviour by smiling back at him. She laughed at the funny thing sticking out of his face that he called a "nose".

"We'll take good care of her," the Nurse promised.

She then turned and wheeled Hope away down the long hospital corridor. Walter held Dawn, and the two of them watched as the little gurney disappeared around the corner. Walter felt Dawn crumple slightly in his arms. He glanced up at the clock; it was eight pm.

* * *

When the clock struck nine, Walter was pacing nervously and drinking a Diet Coke. Dawn was sitting in one of a row of chairs. She held Hope's Baby Book and paged through it for the umpteenth time.

* * *

At ten pm, Dawn was still sitting in the chair, the baby book closed on her lap. She was looking in the direction of the hanging television. On it, Financial Analyst Peter Schiff was forecasting a doom and gloom scenario for the US economy in 2008. Meanwhile, another talking head, by the name of Ben Stein who was best known for playing a bit role in a hit movie called *Ferris Bueller's Day Off*, was now playing the role of a financial expert lambasting Schiff as "simply wrong". Dawn saw this exchange, but to her the words were in a foreign language, and the images simply shadows on a wall.

Walter, after fifteen attempts, had finally persuaded the soft drink machine to take a battered dollar bill. He looked down with satisfaction as a new Diet Coke clattered into the service bin.

* * *

At eleven pm Walter was placing an empty can of Diet Coke at the end of a row of the five previous cans he'd lined up on the magazine table. His hand was shaking slightly from the millions of molecules of caffeine rushing through his blood stream working their psychoactive magic. Dawn, in a trance, was flipping blindly through a copy of Newsweek. They had been joined by a sad clown with his arm in a sling. The clown, in full clown costume and makeup, was waiting for x-ray results to determine whether his arm was broken or not. Either way, one thing was certain, he would never get in that damn cannon again.

* * *

By midnight, the clown was gone. Dawn stood alone in the hallway staring at the clock, waiting for the minute hand to click. There was the sound of a toilet flushing and Walter exited the men's room. He saw Dawn's mesmerized state. She appeared utterly lost, stuck in entropy. He walked up to her and held her tight. Numbly she hugged him back. At first, her grip was loose and weak, but then she gripped him tightly, as if afraid to let go. Walter felt her tears dampen his shoulder. They knew the surgery should have been finished by then.

At one a.m., Walter lifted a shaking hand to deposit another quarter into the soft drink machine. The machine was out of Diet Coke. He considered the other options and wondered what a drink called "Mr. Pibbs" could possibly taste like.

"Mr. and Mrs. Parks?"

Dawn and Walter both turned anxiously. An exhausted surgeon, still in mask and cap, stood in the hallway.

"Is she... ?" Dawn whispered.

They held their collective breath as he untied the mask, revealing a tired smile beneath. "She's going to be fine" he said.

Sheer joy floodlit Walter and Dawn's bodies. Dawn staggered, faint from the sudden release. Walter caught her by the shoulder and held her there. "Oh thank God!" said Dawn.

"Things took a little longer than expected," the Surgeon continued, "but we wanted to do it right."

"It's okay, it's okay..." Dawn gushed.

"Thank you, Doctor," said Walter as he stepped forward to shake the surgeon's hand. "Thank you so much."

"Yes, thank you so much!" Dawn agreed.

"She'll need a couple of days to recover, then you should be able to take her home."

"Really? That soon?" said Dawn.

"Absolutely. However, surgery is very tough on the body and mind, and even more so on the little ones. The best thing you can do for Hope is to take her home where she can be in familiar surroundings and just let her heal."

Walter smiled, "We can do that."

"Can we see her?" Dawn asked anxiously.

"Of course."

* * *

Over the next three days, Walter and Dawn became extremely familiar with the infant ward at Saint Benedict's. At Dawn's request, Walter stopped drinking Diet Coke. This was an easy task to accomplish with Hope out of immediate danger. Bathing, however, was not so easy while essentially living at the hospital. Dawn, in her usual miraculous way, appeared pristine and perfect. Walter, however, took on the air both visual and literal of a homeless man. He was unshaven, his hair matted, and his clothes had that sort of crumpled slept-in look that clothes take on when you do actually sleep in them. Walter didn't mind. He'd never been strong in terms of fashion. Once, when he had made an actual attempt to dress fashionably, a friend had told him that he put the 'dolt' in Dolce Gabbana. Walter, himself, had always been relieved to be male, able to retreat into suits and ties and more or less expected to occasionally spill food items down his shirt. Most of all, however, Walter didn't mind because Hope was getting better. They lived for the brief moments when they could actually hang over the edge of Hope's bassinet and watch the reassuring rhythm of her tiny chest.

*   *   *

The small green Chevy Cavalier turned into the Parks's driveway. Walter glanced back from the driver's seat to where Dawn sat with Hope. Hope, in a silent endorsement of the car's smooth mid-price sedan handling, was fast asleep. "Welcome home, Hope," said Walter cheerfully. He was reminded of the day they'd first brought her home from the hospital. He'd been afraid of every pothole, afraid of his own feet when carrying her. She'd seemed impossibly fragile. She seemed so again now.

Dawn shushed him and carefully lifted their daughter from her car seat. Walter eagerly jumped out and ran to unlock the front door. As he ran up the front steps he noticed two things. The first was how truly badly he needed a bath. The second was a yellow notice hanging on the front door. Walter's heart froze. The official look of the notice, as well as its being actually stapled to the frame made Walter instantly recognize this as a foreclosure notice. That, and the large words "Foreclosure Notice" printed in 32 point type across the top. For a moment, Walter was horrorstruck. He then recovered slightly, only to be horrorstruck again at the thought of the stress this would cause Dawn and, perhaps by some sort emotional osmosis, Hope. Walter wasn't sure how this emotional osmosis would work exactly, but he was quite certain it was possible and definitely not good for recovering babies. He tore off the notice and stuffed it in his pants.

"What was that?" asked Dawn as she carried Hope up the front steps.

"Chinese menu," said Walter. Following his usual compulsion to add minute detail to any lie, he then added, "Ping's House of Sichuan. The food is terrible, you wouldn't like it, which is why I got rid of it. Except the noodles. The Dan Dan noodles are quite good there." Walter paused. He'd gone too far. Dawn liked Dan Dan noodles and might wish to order them, so he quickly added, "But people apparently get food poisoning there a lot. So, we shouldn't order from them. Ever."

Dawn stared at him as if he'd gone completely bonkers, "Why are you telling me this?"

"I have no idea."

Dawn nodded and pushed past him into the house.

* * *

Once Hope was laid into her crib, there was very little to do but continue their vigil, albeit in a different location. Except when needing to be fed or changed, Hope seemed mostly content to sleep. Walter desperately wanted to talk to the Chinese mortgage company but only recalled part of their name and even that he was certain he was misspelling. The only part he remembered clearly was "Wang". This, he discovered, did not produce any bank-related results when Googled. When he finally did locate the bank's website he was further frustrated to find that the only phone numbers were in China, and apparently they didn't want to answer at three a.m. Shanghai time.

Frustrated, he snuck into a closet and called Countricross once more. There, he was reminded by the recorded voice that it was Saturday and he should call back during regular business hours if he even wanted a hope of speaking with a live human being. Walter exited the closet and ran directly into Dawn. "What were you doing in there?" she asked in surprise.

"I'm gay!" he announced, in a vague attempt at humour.

Dawn stared at him, "What were you really doing in there?"

"I needed a moment."

"Okay," she said, apparently accepting this explanation, and walked away.

Walter watched her go, feeling a cocktail of emotions — one part guilt and two parts dread.

* * *

That night Dawn finished feeding Hope and laid her down on the soft white mattress of her crib. Hope smiled contentedly and looked up at her mother from beneath slowly drooping eyelids.

Jesus sniffed about between the slats of Hope's crib. His cold wet nose tickled the baby's toes, causing her to start and giggle. Dawn pushed Jesus away. She then bowed her head in prayer. Quietly she whispered words to God. Finishing on a silent Amen, she opened her own eyes to see that Hope had closed hers. Dawn gently kissed her daughter's forehead and crept out of the room.

* * *

Dawn carefully closed Hope's door behind her. A baby monitor in the living room would allow her to continue to listen in.

Walter sat on the couch watching *The Hills* on TV. It was a show following the lives of very attractive, rich young people from Laguna Beach, California as they struggled with the trials of moving to the Hollywood Hills. He looked up as Dawn entered. "She asleep?"

Dawn nodded and sat beside him on the couch. For a moment she too watched the program before asking, "Why are you watching this?"

"I'm trying to figure out if it's a reality TV show or not."

"Oh."

"It's supposed to be a reality TV show, but I don't think that's possible. I think it's about as real as wrestling."

"You do know the target audience for this is fourteen-year-old girls?"

"Ah right, yes, well, I suppose that makes sense."

For a moment, the two of them watched as the character Lauren was meeting with her boss at Teen Vogue.

"So when were you going to tell me?" asked Dawn, still watching the inane drama.

"That I was watching the Hills?"

"No," said Dawn flatly. "About losing your job? About the foreclosure?"

Walter felt his heart drop straight through his chest, past his feet and land somewhere in the basement next the box of Christmas ornaments. He turned to look at her, but Dawn would not meet his gaze. Lauren's boss was telling the supposed intern that she would be going to Paris. She was assuring Lauren that it would be "hard work". "I didn't want to upset you," Walter explained.

Dawn wasn't intentionally torturing him. That wasn't in her

makeup. She was absorbing and deliberating. Finally, she turned to look at him with fierce eyes. "Walter, I know you think I'm this delicate girl who lives in a perfect church-world and needs to be protected, but I'm not."

It was only the third time Walter had ever seen Dawn genuinely angry. The first time had been when her family "declined" to come to their wedding. The second had been when she'd learned their neighbour Steve had sent a case of 'The Secret' DVDs to poor children in Africa in order to "help them help themselves." She never got angry over material things, such as when Walter had accidentally run her cellphone through the rinse cycle — the first or second time. She only became angry about things that mattered. Walter himself had never felt her anger, and now he melted under it like an ice cube in a microwave.

"I thought you had enough to worry about," he pleaded plaintively.

"I'm your partner. Your *equal* partner. Not some damsel in distress."

Walter put his face in his hands and sobbed, "I know, I'm sorry."

Dawn's anger evaporated, and she gently put a hand on his shoulder. "It's okay. I like that you wanted to protect me. But, you need to know you can't, and shouldn't."

Walter sniffed and rubbed his eyes. She was right, of course, and now that she knew, he was relieved. "How did you find out?" he asked.

"You still don't remember to empty your pants pockets for the laundry," said Dawn as she pulled the folded up foreclosure notice from her pocket. She smiled faintly then turned serious again, "What about our savings? We have savings."

Walter shook his head. There was no point in trying to hide from her the compounded misery of their situation. "Hope's medical costs," he explained.

"What about severance?" she asked, "You were there for years."

"It's all gone. Even with that it was tight."

"Oh my..." was all Dawn could say. Now, the colour drained from her face. Walter watched her reel with the news. He took her hand, but it sat loosely in his grasp. Dawn's normally unshakeable demeanour was gone. Her firmly grounded faith normally made her immune to common stresses. Now, however, she was like a wind blown barn with all its doors banging open and closed. "How long do we have?" she asked numbly.

"A week... maybe."

"Oh Jesus," she said. Jesus perked up at the sound of his name and put his head on her knee. She stared at Walter as a thought struck her, "Hope can't lose her home, Walter, not now."

"I know," said Walter. Walter agreed with the sentiment, but at the same time knew there would be no choice in the matter. The bank would not be interested in their personal problems. Walter then watched as Dawn's thoughts coalesced into resolve as evidenced by the hardening in her eyes.

"We're not leaving," she said. "I don't care what happens. Hope needs her home. *We're not leaving.*"

Walter's first instinct was to argue with her rationally, to reason that there was no fighting the bank, the city, and the inevitable Sheriff's office. Logic said they would have to leave, and their best course of action was to begin investigating some sort of emergency housing arrangement sooner rather than later. Walter opened his mouth to communicate these entirely sensible thoughts. It was then that he met her gaze once more and realized that he was wrong. Without saying a word, Dawn looked at him and sliced through all of his arguments like an electric carving knife through tofu. They loved Hope more than life itself, and right now Hope needed her own home. It wasn't a rational argument. In fact, it completely ignored the many salient points for giving up and leaving. Never-the-less it was right. Walter opened his mouth again, and this time he actually spoke. "We're not leaving," he agreed.

"No matter what?"

"No matter what."

CHAPTER 5

"Let it be." - M. Heidegger

"You need any help, sir?"

Walter glanced over to see the short, stocky Latino clerk from behind the counter smiling helpfully. Walter who had just located the baby food aisle, waved him off. "No, I got it. Thanks!"

Despite being only a mile from his home, Walter had never been inside Cervantes Liquor and Drugs before. Dawn liked to eat healthy and certainly liked Walter and Hope to eat healthy as well. As a result, they had normally patronized the nearby Whole Foods supermarket. Aside from sneaking the occasional McDonald's Big Mac, Walter ate mostly organic food which, as he saw it, would qualify Walter himself as organic. Which is it to say, locally grown and almost entirely free of pesticides.

The sudden change in their economic condition, however had forced them to reexamine the modern luxury of eating locally grown produce. In ancient times, only the wealthy could afford to consume goods imported from the Far East. Today, only the wealthy could afford not to.

Walter looked over the jars of baby food labelled *chicken, carrot* and *apple*. Finally his eyes fell on the lowest shelf, at foot-level, to a disturbingly dusty set of jars labelled *rutabaga*. Walter brushed off the dust. They were on sale and, much to his surprise, had not yet expired.

Moments later, Walter stood at the counter as the diminutive clerk punched up his ten jars of rutabaga pablum. "Your kid must really love rutabaga, huh?" said the clerk cheerfully.

Walter was still in a shell shocked state from the night before. He had thought that telling Dawn the truth would alleviate some of the pressure of keeping it a secret. Instead, he discovered that the preceding relative normality of their homelife had allowed him to deny the hopelessness of the situation. Now, with Dawn aware, her own despair simply reenforced his own sense of calamity. He had promised her that they would not leave the house but had absolutely no notion as to how he would be able to keep that promise. His solution, to date, was to buy cheaper groceries.

"Okay, that's nine-ninety," said the clerk.

Walter who had been busy fantasizing about the possibility of being accidentally sent large quantities of freshly minted cash by the US Treasury, failed to react.

"Sir?" said the clerk. Walter, who was busy wondering at how truly beautiful money in neat stacks bound with elastic bands could be, still failed to respond. The clerk snapped his fingers and said loudly, "Hello sir?"

"Oh, I'm sorry," said Walter, coming back to the reality of ten jars of baby food for ninety-nine cents each. "How much do I owe you?"

"Nine-ninety."

Walter took out his wallet, pulled out nine dollars and began counting coins. "I think I have exact change, one sec..." he said in an emotional stupor.

"Are you okay, sir?"

"What?" said Walter, losing count.

"I'm sorry, it's none of my business," said the clerk.

Walter nodded and began again catatonically counting coins.

"It's just that, I'm really good at telling when someone's upset about something," added the clerk unhelpfully. When Walter looked at him in surprise, the clerk hurriedly added, "But it's none of my business..." Walter nodded once more and began searching his pockets for an additional ten cents. "...that you seem upset," said the clerk, finishing his original sentence.

Walter stopped and examined the clerk. The short Mexican had kind eyes that shone with genuine concern. Walter felt his facade crack, then crumble. "Our baby's sick, I lost my job, and we're about to lose our house. So, no, everything's not all right."

There was a moment of stunned silence as the clerk absorbed this news.

"Oh man. I am so sorry. That sucks. That really, really sucks."

"Yeah," Walter agreed.

"I didn't mean to pry," said the clerk "that truly is none of my business."

"No."

Walter shook his head and resumed counting. The clerk seemed genuinely sorry and had intended no harm.

"But your house, man... Mia Casa is mia casa, you know?"

Walter stared at him once more.

"Oh I'm really sorry man, that was way out of line."

Walter continued to stare at the clerk, but not out of offence. The clerk's words had sparked a tiny ember of thought in Walter's mind, and he was doing his best to blow it into a full fledge flame. Walter's brain; however, being somewhat damp and soggy was not cooperating in the metaphor. Walter smacked himself on the forehead, hoping the same tactic that worked on his television might also apply here. Oddly enough, it did. "No. No, you're right. Mia casa, my castle."

"Actually, mia casa means 'my house'," said the clerk helpfully.

Walter wasn't interested in having his Spanish corrected. His eyes were glazed over with inspiration. "My castle. My home is my castle," he repeated over and over, and then stopped. "I seem to be short ten cents," he said.

"Don't worry about it," said the Clerk.

"Thank you," said Walter. Walter was still deeply enthralled in the primordial thoughts evolving to life in his consciousness. "Thank you very much..."

"Sancho," finished the clerk.

"Sancho," Walter repeated. "Thank you, Sancho." Walter committed the clerk's name to memory. He then drew back into his own thoughts and turned and walked towards the store entrance as if in a trance.

"No problem," Sancho called after him, "but really, it's only ten cents, it's not a big deal."

*   *   *

The Budget Rent-a-Truck turned onto Dream Street and rattled past the Mercedes, BMWs and Lexuses parked in their respective driveways. It was the largest vehicle size available from the company. Never-the-less the truck's tires were compressed under the weight of its load.

Steve Prefect was busy driving his John Deer riding mower in lines up and down the length of his front lawn. Steve secretly liked to imagine each dandelion he cut down was a little person crying out "No! No!" and that he was a merciless old world god smiting them. He had even given himself a name, *Megwah*. Sometimes he would pause for just a moment to hear their imagined pleas before driving over them with relish, demanding they thank him even for that brief respite. Steve had confessed his godlike fantasies only once, after too many martinis while standing at a Men's room urinal during an investors' conference. The older man beside him told Steve that he knew exactly what he meant and that there was nothing wrong with it. "We're all Megwah," the man had said. The next day, hungover and worried, Steve could only remember the man's first name, 'Bernie'. He worried some days that Bernie had been mocking him and that his secret fantasies would be revealed, but they never were.

Steve looked up in surprise at the large rent-a-truck rumbling down their street. His surprise grew as the truck turned into Walter's driveway. When the door opened and Walter himself stepped down, Steve's surprise turned to a mixture of presumption and delight. Clearly it was *time*. Walter was moving out. The only puzzling element was the strange expression on Walter's face. It looked oddly like a smile. In fact, Walter appeared to be beaming with delight. Steve surmised that his neighbour had simply cracked under the pressure. It was all very sad, thought Steve with a smirk, as he tried to imagine Walter as a dandelion. "Moving out already?" Steve said unto him. "Can't say I'm sorry to not have your dog crapping on my lawn anymore, but no hard feelings, hmm?"

Walter looked at Steve with the same, somewhat unsettling smile and answered, "I'm telling you, Steve, that wasn't Jesus, and, no, we're not going anywhere."

Walter turned and headed around to the back of the truck. Steve followed on his mower. "Uh-huh. I saw the notice on your door, Walter," he said, then added, "Very sad."

"Thanks for taking an interest, Steve, I really appreciate it."

Walter was still failing to cooperate. His sarcasm betrayed only mild annoyance, rather than the complete misery Steve had been anticipating. Steve played his trump card, "Plus, you forget, I'm in the mortgage-backed securities biz, so I have access to people's personal financial records. You're in serious trouble. You lost your job, you have no money, your house is underwater..."

For a moment, Steve thought he detected a tremor at the corner of Walter's mouth and the stiffening of his jaw. Amazingly, however,

Walter was able to recover his bearing, although he turned and resolutely focused on opening the trailer doors.

Sensing an opening, Steve pressed his perceived advantage, "Still, I am willing to help you out. I am prepared to make a very generous offer on your house, right here, right now."

Steve took a sheet of paper from his pocket and handed it to Walter. He watched with satisfaction the appalled look that crept over his neighbour's face. "This is less than half what we paid for it a year ago," said Walter.

"Yeah, well, beggars can't be choosers," grinned Steve. "I'd really be doing you a favour."

"Me a favour? By handing me the hemlock? No thanks."

Walter swung open the trailer doors, satisfactorily hiding Steve from sight. He began conducting an inventory of the truck's contents.

Steve, not willing to miss out on the delight of watching Walter squirm, dismounted from his mower and stepped back into sight. "Market's going down Walter, this could be the best offer you get. You don't know what I know."

"Do you know what you know?"

"What?" Steve paused to consider what that meant and decided it meant nothing. "Don't be stupid, Walter, I'm doing you a favour."

"So what? I'll be a little less bankrupt? Anyway, as I said we're not going anywhere."

Steve shook his head. Clearly, Walter was in denial. Steve had come to believe that the only people with the true analytical perspective to understand the world were, in fact, investment bankers. Only they had the cold insight and lofty presence of mind required to see the truth at all times. The enormous profits they made, he felt, was the proof of their perceptive preeminence.

Walter reached into the back of the truck and carefully lifted something. "Can you hold this for me?" he asked.

Steve, entwined in the delight of the moment, simply held out his hands and said, "Well, unless you won the–"

Walter handed Steve an enormous cement cinder block. Steve, caught by surprise, let the heavy object slip through his fingers and crash to the asphalt inches from his own feet. "Jesus Christ, you almost broke my frickin'toes!"

"Oh gosh, I am sorry about that," said Walter, flashing again that annoying smile.

Steve didn't think Walter was sorry at all. He pulled wide the nearest truck door, "What the Hell are you doing anyway...?"

Steve stared in baffled wonder at the contents of the trailer. It wasn't empty for moving at all, as he had assumed. Instead, the interior was stacked high with cinder blocks, bags of cement, wooden beams and other building materials.

"What are you doing?" demanded Steve.

"I'll tell you one more time, *we're not going anywhere.*"

His inventory complete, Walter closed the trailer doors and walked towards his front door. Steve for a moment stared after him, flabbergasted. It was as if one of the dandelions had leapt up onto his lawnmower and poured sugar into the gas tank. Steve opened his mouth in protest, but no words came out. At the same moment, both men noticed Jesus, squatting on Steve's lawn.

"Ah ha! See? See? I knew it!" said Steve with vindication.

"You're absolutely right," agreed Walter. Walter then whistled, and Jesus gleefully scampered over to greet him. "Good boy," said Walter, scratching his ears.

"You gonna clean this up?" demanded Steve.

"Nope," said Walter who then, before his neighbour could respond, disappeared into his house with the dog.

CHAPTER 6

"The fifth? The fifth works for me..." - B. Juárez

Sancho handed the old woman her change, smiled and said "Thank you, have a good day." While this sort of thing is routinely said by clerks and telemarketing machines the world over with about equal enthusiasm, Sancho always meant it and his customers knew it. His own sincerity often meant he mistook the same in others. People would frequently ask him how he was doing and, much to their surprise, he would reply by telling them exactly how he was doing. This was almost always "very well," but the sincere directness of his response would often leave them eying him suspiciously as perhaps some sort of retrograde or even sociopath.

The old woman smiled back and left with her groceries.

Walter Parks stepped up to the counter in her place. "Hello," he said. Walter was smiling broadly.

"Hey-hey! My friend, you look like you got your house back." Sancho was genuinely pleased for Walter.

Walter eyed him suspiciously, but decided the clerk truly meant it. "Maybe. Well, sort of."

"We'll you look one hundred times better. The last time you came in here you had the look of a man defeated — taken down by life. Today, you look like a man who has taken his life back. A conquistador!" Sancho waved an imaginary sword. "Ha! Ha!"

"Yes, thank you," Walter agreed. He hadn't realized how evident his new found purpose was. Having accepted Sancho's enthusiasm as authentic, he found the clerk's energy invigorating.

"So... what can I help you with? Your baby needs more zucchini pablum?"

"It was rutabaga and no, we're fine."

"Good." For a moment, the conversation reached an impasse. Walter wasn't asking for anything to purchase. Still, he had clearly approached the counter with intention. Sancho thought, perhaps he does not understand the purpose of a store, although that seemed unlikely. Walter didn't appear to be an idiot and had shopped there successfully before. "So..." Sancho prompted.

"So, Sancho, I have an odd question for you."

"Okay..." said Sancho. People didn't normally enter the story to ask him questions other than, "How are you doing?" even though they often seemed oddly suspicious no matter how sincerely he answered them. The only other questions concerned the products themselves, such as "how many beans are in a can?" and "can I take this shampoo orally?"

Walter continued, "I hope you won't be offended. It's just that... well, you are Mexican aren't you?"

"That is true and not at all offensive," Sancho gladly replied, "I am a very proud Mexican."

"Right, I know. What I wanted to know is, can you tell me where I can find any... day labourers."

"Illegals?" said Sancho, clearly shocked, "You want illegals? You think because I am Mexican I know illegal immigrants? You think my whole family perhaps is illegal?"

"Um..."

"What, are you with the ICE?" said Sancho. He was not referring to the frozen cubes of water available in bags for two dollars in the store freezer but rather to the United States Immigration and Customs Enforcement agency. As with its nonacronym homonym, however, the agency could cause the blood to freeze in people's veins. Sancho being a legal US resident, complete with green card, theoretically had nothing to fear from any ICE agent. Still, within the Mexican community, such agents had the sort of legendary status normally reserved for mythical creatures such as werewolves or nonCuban Latino Republicans.

"No," said Walter firmly.

Sancho studied him for a moment, then picked up the phone. "Okay, I'll call my cousin."

* * *

Walter walked down the line of illegal immigrants on his front lawn as if he were a general inspecting his troops. The men came in every shape and size; tall, short, fat, and thin. They generally wore jeans and loose fitting collared shirts or T's. They each looked at Walter with eyes of hope. All of these men needed the work, and their hope was that Walter would pick them. Walter wasn't used to being in such a position. Normally, the only time he ever got to choose people or issue orders was when he played with his miniature knights. It was an odd feeling, he noted, but not an unpleasant one.

Of course, Walter had thought about hiring Americans to help him with his grand scheme. However, having not enough cash to pay for his outstanding mortgage, he certainly did not have enough to pay an American company. What's more, he had noticed that whenever he'd hired an American contractor in the past, the workers who arrived to do the work looked exactly the same as the ones standing before him now.

Walter nodded as he passed each man and said, "Good". He had little criteria for whom he hired. The project would have to be done quickly and cheaply. As long as the men appeared physically capable of holding a hammer, they were hired. "Good... good... good..." Walter continued as he walked. Walter then stopped in surprise. The man standing before him didn't look very Mexican. Walter glanced back at the men he'd passed with their black hair and tanned complexions. This man was tall, reedy, and very blond. Walter considered the likelihood of a tall blond Latino and, while no ethnologist, decided he was quite certain this man was not from anywhere south of the United States at all.

Walter considered how to address the issue. He didn't want to appear antiwhite, had many white friends, and of course, was a caucasian himself. "Um, what is..."

"Olaf," Olaf offered with a smile.

"Thank you. What is Olaf doing here?"

Sancho shrugged. "You said you wanted illegal immigrant workers, Olaf is here from Sweden... illegally."

"Ja, is true," confirmed Olaf with a now distinct Swedish accent. "My visa, it has expired."

"I see," said Walter.

"I'm a goot with mine hands," said Olaf, "I used to built furniture in Sweden."

"Of course you did," said Walter. The man looked at him with watery blue eyes that were most unMexican, but equally full of hope. "Okay, good," said Walter.

Olaf grinned with relief. "Goot," he agreed, "Bra."

Walter continued down the line of more conventional migrant workers, "Good, good, good, good, good, good."

As he reached the end of the line, Sancho who had been walking along side of him, stepped forward and joined it. "Sancho what are you doing?" asked Walter with surprise.

"I'm offering my services," said Sancho. Walter had explained the objective of his endeavour to Sancho; who had listened with even more than his usual enthusiasm.

"Yes, but you have a job, and a green card."

"Si, and I sell gum and lottery tickets, but for what?" Sancho asked. "You, sir, are standing for something. You are a man fighting for what you believe in."

"Um..." said Walter, utterly failing to grasp the moment.

"This is a cause, sir, a quest, and I want to be a part of it. Your fight, is my fight."

"Really?" said Walter with disbelief. Walter had never inspired anyone before. He had received positive performance reviews at work and had even been given an occasional 'Exceeded Expectations', but this was quite different. Sancho was excited by what Walter wanted to accomplish. It was another odd feeling, but also a pleasant one.

"Yes, really."

"Well, thank you, Sancho," said Walter.

For a moment, the two men regarded one another. For Sancho it was a moment of deep understanding of the potential magnitude of what they were going to do. For Walter, it was an awkward pause as he tried to figure out what to say next. "Did you tell them what we're building?" asked Walter.

"No, sir, I did not."

Walter nodded, okay, now he had something to say. He turned and faced the line of fifteen expectant faces. "Gentlemen, thank you all for coming."

The faces looked at him with mostly blank expressions as if he had just read them instructions for making soup. Walter immediately began to doubt his ability to lead.

Sancho translated Walter's words and the faces nodded with understanding and even smiled. Walter was relieved and continued, "What we are building here is this..."

Once Sancho had translated, with a flourish Walter held up his *Castles of Europe* calendar.

There was a look of bafflement on several of the faces before one of the workers asked, in broken English, "Why you need so many men to build a calendar?"

"No, no," insisted Walter tapping the photo on the page, "*this*." The picture Walter tapped was the December photo of the splendiferous Warwick Castle in England, with its soaring towers and snow covered parapets. "But smaller," he explained, "And without all the snow."

* * *

Over the next several days Walter, Sancho, the Mexicans and one Swede threw themselves into the project.

First, a deep trench was dug around the property, circumscribing the lot. During this time, several of Walter's neighbours approached him curiously and asked what he was doing. Walter would tell them that it was to do with the septic system. "I've been dealing with a lot of crap," he would say. Since it was a large trench, the neighbours would accept this and walk away. Everyone that is, except Steve. Steve didn't know what Walter was doing either, but he was determined to stop it.

The second step was to chop down the 'American Dream' billboard on the front lawn. The lawn would become the "ward" of the castle and space was limited, so the sign would have to go. Walter reasoned that violating his agreement with the Plansville developers would be the least of his concerns.

All of the construction had to be done as quietly as possible. Since the goal was to keep Hope comfortable in her own home, disturbing the baby's sleep was counterproductive. Walter instructed the men to use sign language and whispers to communicate, to put cloth over hammerheads and so on. This had the added benefit of disturbing the neighbours less who were then more inclined to ignore whatever they were doing. Except Steve, of course, who would stop by to shout and wave his arms at Walter whenever possible. Walter would then send one of the Mexicans who did not speak English over to negotiate. This only infuriated Steve more.

The third stage involved constructing the wall frame in wood. Walter hadn't the money to pay for all of the construction materials needed for the project. He had been forced to rely on that wonderful invention known as the credit card. Credit cards are, of course, a magical piece of numbered plastic that allows you to buy something for nothing, provided you intend to move to Bolivia before the bill is due. Otherwise, they have the reverse effect, allowing the bank to charge earth-shattering interest in the range of a Las Vegas leg-breaker. In reality, the basic business model of the credit card is where the bank acts as a bar owner who offers to buy free first drinks for alcoholics. The bank only really makes money from customers who become dependent on them or 'can't hold their liquor'. It is a true fact that in the credit card business world, customers who actually pay their bills in full, on time, every time, are referred to as "deadbeats". Of course, this business model has one flaw, in this case that flaw would be Walter Parks. A customer who doesn't care if he goes bankrupt or not, simply isn't part of the equation. The idea is to keep the alcoholics drunk, not to allow them to go off and hang themselves from the pipes in the men's room ceiling without paying their bills. To make matters more ironic, Walter's credit card was a Visa card issued by a bank owned in part by the Wang Hui Tau Bank of Hong Kong. So the bank was effectively funding his own plans to thwart them. "Ha! Ha!" thought Walter as he'd swiped the card at Home Depot.

Each day, twice a day, Dawn would walk around the construction site providing lemonade and cookies to the workers and Walter. The men grew to know her and Hope and worked with a vigour money could not buy. With the frame complete, the men began work laying the cinder block wall. Soon, Steve Prefect's angry protests were reduced to a pair of waving hands hidden behind a concrete barrier.

Walter's next challenge was to buy supplies. By this time, his credit card had "maxed out" and he needed to preserve his small reserve of cash to pay the men. Fortunately, he found that he could easily get a new store credit card, receive one hundred dollars off of his purchase and continue to spend to oblivion. What Walter was beginning to realize was that, in the analogy of the banks as bartenders, the bartender couldn't resist his own merchandise, making the whole enterprise an Alcoholics Unanimous meeting. Walter arrived back at the house with food supplies, drinking water and barrels of gasoline.

At the end of the first week, a municipal official appeared bearing a cease-and-desist notice. Steve, who had notified the city of Walter's unpermitted proceedings, watched with satisfaction as the man, whose name was Doug, handed Walter the official document. Doug, who had been handing out such notices for years, told Walter that his was the most egregious violation of city laws he'd ever seen.

"Oh yes?" said Walter.

"Yes," said Doug who appeared more impressed than outraged. He asked Walter what exactly he was building.

"A castle," Walter replied. The two men laughed and laughed until Walter said, "No, I'm serious."

This prompted the two men to laugh some more until finally Doug said, "It's okay, you don't have to tell me if you don't want to." Normally, homeowners who were halted in the midst of home improvements were angry or at least sad. Doug was delighted by Walter's easygoing response to the intervention. Walter cheerfully signed for his receipt of the document and Doug, having accomplished his task, prepared to leave. It was at that point that Steve confronted Doug demanding that the official understand his distress. Doug pointed out that, as a city official, he wasn't required to "understand anything at all" and left. As Steve scowled angrily at Walter, Walter smiled back and filed the cease-and-desist notice into a rented wood chipper.

On the tenth day Walter halted construction so the men could watch as he ceremoniously switched on the tap, sending a stream of water down a hose and initiating the process of flooding the trench. One of his neighbours, Mr. Holbrook, noticed the rising tide in the trench and pointed out that Walter appeared to be having problems with his new septic system. Walter looked at the rising moat, then looked at the Mr. Holbrook, agreed and thanked him sincerely for his input.

The only serious disruption in the project occurred when an unmarked van roared up, and a contingent of ICE officers raided the site. The Mexicans fled over neighbouring fences and yards leaving Walter and Olaf staring about in surprise. Steve, who had, of course, called the immigration officers, stared in disbelief as not a single worker was successfully apprehended. None thought to ask Olaf for his papers. When the officers prepared to leave, Steve demanded they take action on what was now clearly a castle under construction. The officers pointed out that this was far out of their jurisdiction and suggested Steve file a complaint with the city. An hour later, as Steve watched, the labourers returned, and work resumed once again.

At the end of the second week worked halted again, this time for good. Under the night sky, by the flickering light of tiki torches, Walter and the others stood by as Sancho proudly placed the last stone. "It is done," said Sancho.

"Yup," said Walter. Walter then turned to the men and said, "How does Pizza sound? Is everyone okay with Pizza?"

CHAPTER 7

"Government is not a solution to our problem,
government is the problem." - O. Bin Laden

"He's completely insane!" shouted Steve.

Steve was pacing furiously in Ralph Emerson's office. Ralph Emerson's office was in the Municipal Department of Housing. Ralph Emerson himself was in his office, behind his desk, watching Steve's face turn as red as a beet and pondering whether a man's head could actually explode from internal pressure.

"He and his bible belt crazy wife are completely loco! Do you understand?" Steve continued.

Ralph calmly took a sip of his coffee and counted to three. He'd read somewhere that counting to three could calm someone down who was angry, although he had a nagging suspicion it was Steve who should be doing the counting. "No, Mr. Prefect, but I do understand that you're upset. If you want to file a grievance, I recommend you–"

"I've already filed a grievance!" shouted Steve, throwing up his arms in exasperation.

"Well then, that should start a process which–"

"Nothing happened."

Steve leaned forward over Ralph's desk, positioning his burning red visage inches from Ralph's. Ralph could feel the heat of Steve's fury and noted the large vein that throbbed disturbingly in Steve's temple. It reminded Ralph of the aliens from the television pilot of Star Trek. Ralph wondered if, like the aliens, Steve could see into his mind. "One... two... three..." said Ralph.

"What are you doing?" yelled Steve.

Ralph had hoped that counting aloud might make the difference. "Nothing," he said.

"Exactly!" said Steve. "Just like your department."

Ralph swallowed and opened the file folder on his desk. "No," said Ralph with forced calm, "according to my records we did take action. We presented him with a cease-and-desist order last week. Of course, if he fails to comply within the next eight weeks, then we can–"

"He put it in a wood chipper."

"I'm sorry?" said Ralph.

"He put your damn order into a wood chipper," said Steve.

"He put our paperwork in a wood chipper?" replied Ralph. The idea of someone destroying official city documents was absurd. It was unacceptable, possibly illegal, and certainly sacrilegious.

"Yup."

"Intentionally?"

"Brrr-veeet!" said Steve as he made a motion with his hand like a sheet of paper shooting up through a shredding chute.

It took Ralph a moment to absorb this flagrant disrespect of city ordinances. He considered, for a moment, counting to three then dismissed the idea. "We'll see about that," he fumed.

Steve watched with satisfaction as Ralph's expression flushed with gratifying anger and a tiny vein began to throb in the city official's forehead.

* * *

Steve hunched forward in the back seat of the Sheriff's car. Had the cage not prevented him, he would have stuck his head between the front seats to better communicate his thoughts to the Sheriff, who drove, and Ralph, who sat in the passenger seat. "Turn right here," Steve shouted at the police officer.

"I know where I'm going, Mr. Prefect."

Steve's anger had transformed into excitement. The presence of the Sheriff meant that Walter's party was about to end. Walter would either cease and desist, and his new residence would be the city jail. Jesus, would also have to go, he thought, taken to the city pound where he could delightfully die for Walter's sins.

"They're all crazy," Steve assured them. "Walter, his wife, the dog, even the baby, I bet."

The Sheriff studied Steve's maniacal expression in the rear view mirror. "Uh huh," he said, "And you say they've built a castle?" The

Sheriff wasn't at all sure whom he might be arresting that day.

"They're crazy!" said Steve and then added for clarity, "Cra-a-a-azy!"

"I see."

Ralph wasn't sure what to believe. All he knew was that the documents were either in danger or destroyed and that one way or another someone would have to fill out the proper paperwork explaining how.

"Oh, here! Turn here!" Steve shouted again.

The Sheriff, who had been about to turn anyway, did so with a sharp scowl.

* * *

At that moment Walter Parks was standing in Dream Street facing the long line of illegal immigrants whom he had come to consider as friends. He walked down the line shaking each man's hand and handing over a wad of cash. "Thank you. Thank you all so much," he said.

"Our pleasure, Señor," said the first worker, whose name was Manuel.

"Si," agreed Julio.

The others, many of who did not understand the exchanges but sensed the sentiment, nodded their heads in agreement.

Olaf, unable to control himself, hugged Walter in a teary embrace. "Sank you! Sank you!" he gushed.

Walter pried himself from the sobbing Swede. "No, Olaf, sank you, I mean, thank *you*."

Finally, Walter reached the end of the line where Sancho stood with a stalwart stance. "And you, I don't know how to thank you enough"

"I'm not going anywhere, Mr. Parks," stated Sancho.

Walter smiled sadly. He appreciated the gesture, but he knew he could neither afford nor ask for further assistance. "Sancho, thank you, but the work here is done. Things are going to get very difficult, very soon. They're going to try to kick us out, and we're not leaving."

"I understand," said Sancho flatly.

Walter was stunned. He knew his charismatic leadership skills couldn't be responsible for this kind of loyalty as he knew he hadn't any. Still, the look in Sancho's eyes was clear and certain. "Sancho, you need to go," said Walter firmly.

"No, I need to stay. I told you. I want to do something that means something. Su casa es mi casa."

"Sancho..." Walter wasn't sure what Sancho meant by "something that means something". He thought of asking Sancho to explain at least one of the "somethings".

"Policía!" shouted Julio as he pointed to the crown of the Sheriff's car just visible down the length of Dream Street.

"Okay, run! Thank you all!" shouted Walter.

The men all waved and smiled back before sprinting off in different directions, over fences, and down the street away from the approaching cruiser.

In seconds only Walter and Sancho remained standing in the street. "Are you sure you know what you're doing?" said Walter.

"Are you?" asked Sancho.

"Touché"

* * *

All three men leaned forward in the Sheriff's police cruiser as they approached what used to be the Parks's house on Dream Street.

"Holy Christ's boxer shorts!" shouted the Sheriff.

"I told you," said Steve.

The entire lot was encircled by a moat filled with water. The moat enclosed a fifteen-foot high concrete wall, complete with parapets and towers topped with red pennants flapping in the morning breeze. Beyond that, the roof of the Parks's family home and DirecTV satellite dish were just barely visible.

"That's not to code. That's not to code at all..." gasped Ralph.

Walter and Sancho stood out on the street and watched them approach for a moment. Walter then waved and the two men retreated over the moat and through the castle gate via a small drawbridge. Once across, Walter tapped a garage door remote and the drawbridge slowly cranked closed behind them.

The Sheriff stopped his car directly in front and the three men stepped out. The Sheriff drew his gun. Ralph slunk back into the passenger's seat. Steve delighted in the prospect that someone, preferably Walter, might be shot.

By this point several neighbours had stepped out of their homes to watch. Since this was a work day, most of the neighbours who had jobs weren't home. This meant that the audience primarily consisted of housewives and small children who had decided that daytime dramas and Sesame Street weren't nearly as interesting as the kind of live action theatre taking place before them—the kind where guns were drawn. A series of excited murmurs and exchanged glances greeted the sight of exposed gunmetal.

"You see? You see what I was saying?" Steve ranted at the Sheriff and Ralph. Steve pointed vigorously at the castle walls on the off-chance they hadn't noticed them. "He's completely insane! Completely! He's not playing by the rules anymore. It's as if he said, oh I don't like this game, so I'm making up my own rules."

The Sheriff looked Steve squarely in the eye. "Mr. Prefect, I advise you to exercise your first amendment rights to shut your pie-hole."

Steve opened his mouth to protest, thought better of it, and closed it once more.

The Sheriff considered wading into the water, but he'd worn his own shoes to work that day and decided against it. Besides, he realized, he had no means to scale the walls even if he did. He had rope in the trunk of the car, but had never been a good climber. Even as a child in gym class he'd struggled with climbing. The other kids would taunt him and yell "Fatty, fatty two-by-four..." Of course, his greatest pleasure now was stopping his former classmates and giving them tickets for driving two miles per hour over the speed limit. All of this, he realized, was beside the point. He glanced about. At least two members of the crowd had out cellphones and another had an actual handheld video recorder. Nothing cramped the style of old time police work like the threat of YouTube. The Sheriff patted down his hair and straightened his collar. He then picked up a small stone from the side of the road and threw it at the drawbridge. It rebounded off with a loud "thwack!".

Inside Jesus began to bark. A tiny peephole door opened in the wood and Walter Parks looked out. "Hello?"

"Mr. Parks..." The Sheriff's voice cracked in a higher pitch than intended. He cleared his throat and began again in a lower register, "Mr. Parks. I'd like to speak with you, I advise you to come outside immediately and cooperate."

"Or what?" asked Walter.

The Sheriff noted that Walter's tone was non confrontational. It was as if he really had no idea what the alternatives were. "Or we'll be forced to come inside."

"Do you have a warrant?"

"No," the Sheriff admitted, silently cursing YouTube. "But we have probable cause."

"Probable cause of what?"

"Of a crime!" said the Sheriff with frustration. He forced himself to stay calm.

"Of what crime?"

"Of violating city code!" shouted Ralph from the car.

"Violating city code is a crime?" said Walter.

"It could be..." said the Sheriff weakly.

"Of being an asshole!" shouted Steve.

The Sheriff cast him a withering glance. "Look, Mr. Parks, let's be reasonable."

"I'd rather not," said Walter. "It hasn't really been working out for me."

The Sheriff was unsure how to proceed. "You know we'll be able to get a warrant, and then we can come in and arrest you."

"You can try."

"Try what? Getting a warrant or arresting you?"

"Both."

"Are you resisting arrest?" said the Sheriff seeing an opportunity.

"Not until you have a warrant to arrest me," said Walter, then added "I'm a bit of a stickler for proper procedures."

"That seems fair enough," agreed Ralph.

"Fine," the Sheriff grumbled, "We'll be back." He then slid his pistol back into its holster and walked back to the car.

"See you then," said Walter and he slid the peephole door closed.

"Is that it?" shouted Steve indignantly.

"For now," said the Sheriff.

Steve then stomped about in angry circles as the Sheriff sat in the driver's seat and called for backup.

CHAPTER 8

"Hey look, I'm on TV!" - M. McLuhan

WKZK, Channel 8 in New Jersey was one of those rare truly independent stations in America. It wasn't an affiliate of any network nor a member of any group of "independents". WKZK, in its squat beige brick offices off the interstate, stood alone. Of course, there had been attempts to acquire it by ABC, CBS, NBC, and, more recently Fox, but its reclusive owner, Samuel Praxton, never responded to any such entreats. WKZK had been founded in the 1960s as a local television station. In 1994 it had been bought by a man named Glen Goldwright who had a vision of jumping on the specialty channel bandwagon and redubbed the station *The Obituary Channel* or *Obit-TV*. His theory went like this; old people often turn first to the obituaries when reading their newspaper and old people also watch a lot of television, therefore a channel dedicated to this apparently fascinating subject would be "a surefire hit". Of course, in practical terms this translated to nonstop funeral processions, cremations, and the scattering of ashes. Morning programming included a show called *Wakey Wakey* in which nobody did any actual waking up. We're putting the "*fun* back in funeral," Goldsmith tried to explain to advertisers. The best Goldsmith could manage, however, were a few deals with morticians, memorial makers and tobacco companies. Advertisers, it seemed, had little desire to associate their brands with death. His second attempt was called *The Surfing Channel*. With a target demographic of men, it showed thirty-second clips of what was currently playing on other channels. When that also failed, Goldsmith sold the station to its current owner, Samuel Praxton. Praxton seemed to have no grand scheme for WKZK. He simply let it revert to its previous format of inexpensive reruns of old shows and one produced program, the local news. Its reach was small and its audience smaller. So WKZK Channel 8 remained independent but largely insignificant, which was, not coincidentally, exactly how Channel 8 news reporter, Sheila Blitz, felt most of the time.

"You wanted to see me, Dan?" asked Sheila, leaning into Dan's office.

"Yeah, yeah," said Dan. He waved her in without looking up from the stacks of papers piled on his desk.

Sheila entered and sat down in the creaky swivel chair opposite him. Dan Whitely was the station manager and her boss. Nobody except Dan ever had contact with the station owner, the elusive Mr. Praxton. Even Dan only ever received communication in the form of phone calls or signed letters. The fact was, no one actually knew what Samuel Praxton looked like. It was rumoured that he monitored the station through an alternate identity as one of the janitors. Sheila suspected that Sam Praxton himself may have started the rumour to keep them all on their toes. She couldn't believe the millionaire was nearly as interesting as people imagined him to be. Would an interesting man want to own a station where the top story of the year was about the expansion of a local bread company? Sheila rolled her eyes at the plaque commemorating that fact hanging on the wall behind Dan's head. Craig Mathews, the reporter on that showpiece of journalistic achievement, had managed to work fourteen puns into the fifteen minutes of actual airtime. These included "rising prospects", "an upper crust product", "panning out" and so on. The real reason his story had won, Sheila was certain, was because it was a feel-good story about local people getting jobs in a year when most weren't.

Dan thanked the caller and hung up the phone shaking his head, "I swear only nuts write letters anymore. We cover the municipal elections, and now I'm stuck with a truckload of mail complaining that we're either too far left or we're too far right."

"Well, are we?"

"Are we what?"

"Are we too far left or too far right?"

Dan looked at Sheila as if a small creature had just crawled out of her nose. "Jesus, Sheila, you might as well ask an ice cream shop if it's pro-chocolate or pro-vanilla. We're pro-whatever sells."

To Dan, there was no mystery or magic in the station. Praxton demanded it make money. Not much money perhaps, but a little. Of course, when the only shows you can afford to air include *Mr. Terrific*, *The Adventures of Brisco County Jr.* and *Muppets Tonight* trying to attract on audience beyond the diminutive demographic of fans of failed TV programs becomes a nearly impossible task. The local news was their most expensive show, but it was also by far their most watched, and Dan would do whatever it took to keep it that way. That was why he ran it after *Tenspeed and Brown Shoe*, the only show they had that actually included a second season.

"Right, but what about journalistic integrity?" Sheila asked.

Dan almost choked on his coffee. The small creature that had metaphorically crawled out of Sheila's nose had now begun to dance the Macarena on her upper lip. "What are you talking about?" he asked, wiping the dribbled drink from his chin.

"Nothing," said Sheila, letting it go. "You wanted to see me about something?"

"Oh right," said Dan. He held up his finger as he fished about his desk for the note he'd been handed minutes earlier. "Apparently there's some sort of 'domestic disturbance' taking place in that Plansville development off Kilter Road." Finding the note he glanced it over, confirming the facts and handed it to Sheila. "Take one of the guys down with the sat-truck."

"You want me to cover it live?"

"Yup, for six o'clock. There's some murmurs on the wire that it might be *something*, whatever that means."

"Really?" Sheila asked with growing excitement. Sheila had never actually done a live feed before. Dan usually eschewed the cost of the satellite feed.

"Yeah, well, don't get too excited," smiled Dan. "Even odds says it's over before you arrive. Anyhoo just get your pretty little butt down there and do what you do."

"Do what I do?"

"Sell us some ice cream."

*　*　*

Bob, the cameraman, drove while Sheila adjusted her makeup in the vanity mirror. Bob looked like a man who only ever wanted to be behind the camera. His curly long hair and plaid lumberjack jacket made him look more like a rock 'n' roll roadie than newscrew member. He also had that acerbic outlook of someone who is never in charge and bitter about it. "Everyone here is stupid," he'd say. "What about you?" someone would ask. "Especially me," he'd reply, "I keep working for 'em."

"All that effort for another crappy story no one cares about," said Bob.

"You don't know that," said Sheila trying not to poke out her eye with eyeliner.

"Of course I do, it's local news! Who cares? Someone forgot to pay their library dues, whoopee!"

"Ha, ha, ha," said Sheila. "No, it's some sort of domestic disturbance, and apparently it might be... something."

"Something boring," said Bob. "Sheila, I know you need to believe that all of this matters and someday you'll be discovered by one of the networks, but let me remind you; nothing worthy of national coverage ever happens here. It's like... a rule or something."

"Well, you never know," said Sheila removing the cap from her lipstick and pouting into the mirror.

"Yeah, I know," said Bob turning onto Dream Street. "I know that covering local news in Plansville is like covering weather in Palm Springs. Ever day is as dull as–"

At that moment, Bob saw something that made him slam the brakes in surprise. The sudden stop made Sheila scrawl a long line in *Cherry-Pop Rouge* across her cheek.

"Jeez, Bob, look what you made me–"

Sheila saw the look of astonishment on Bob's face. She then followed his gaze past the windshield and flipped the vanity up to see. "What are...? Oh, wow." It took a moment for her brain to process the incongruity — house, house, castle, house. Castle, she thought, well that's... *something*.

CHAPTER 9

"I think I liked the chairs the way we had them before."
- Capt. Ed Smith

Jesus bounded after the stick with unbridled enthusiasm. "It's a stick!" he thought, "Or perhaps a very thin squirrel. Either way, could there be anything more exciting?" Actually, Jesus didn't so much think, as do. That would be his life philosophy, if he actually thought about it, which he didn't.

"They're going to come back, you know?" said Sancho to Walter as the two men watched Walter's dog race across the lawn. It was now twilight and the lights from the house cast long shadows along the grass.

"I know," said Walter.

Jesus caught the stick on the first bounce. "Yes!" he might have thought, had he. Then, he might have thought, "Wait, that wall didn't use to be there," just before crashing into it. Jesus had actually crashed into the newly constructed castle wall several times, but long term memory was not his strong suit. The repeated impacts probably hadn't helped either. It didn't matter much. He shook his head after the impact and bounded back to Walter, stick in mouth and ready for more.

"They're going to bring more police with them," said Sancho soberly.

"I know," said Walter as he pried the slobber soaked stick from Jesus's mouth. Jesus quivered with anticipation.

"They will knock down these walls, and they will take your home. They think you are a crazy fool."

Walter nodded and threw the stick.

Jesus took off like a shot, "It's a stick..." he might have thought. Once more the dog caught the stick and, again, collided into the castle wall.

"Jesus is going to hurt himself," said Sancho, pronouncing the dog's name "Hey Zeus".

"He's tougher than that," said Walter. "And it's Jesus, not Hey Zeus." Jesus returned again with equal enthusiasm. Walter looked at the dog who looked back at him expectantly. "A poet once said that, to a dog, there is no such thing as a fool's errand."

"Yes, but your dog also eats his own caca," said Sancho.

"True," said Walter as he threw the stick again.

At that moment a helicopter roared overhead, paused a moment, then continued on. Both men stared after it in shock. Jesus began barking ferociously at the sky.

"Was that the police?" stammered Sancho.

"I think it was a news helicopter."

"I run up and see!" shouted Sancho and he turned and raced towards the front wall. There, he scrambled up a ladder to look out over the parapets.

Walter jogged up behind and called up to him, "Well, can you see anything?"

"Sir, I think you better come look for yourself."

Walter climbed up the ladder with apprehension and looked over the top of the wall. "Oh my..." was all he could say.

Dream Street was now full of people. Crowds of neighbours and others pressed against police barricades to gain a better view of the castle. The Sheriff's car had returned, joined by a half-dozen other cruisers and a large mobile operations van. Police officers scrambled to direct the crowd and set up new police lines and floodlights. Two helicopters were visible hovering high in the sky.

For a moment, everyone on the street were so intent on what each other was doing that no one noticed Walter and Sancho looking out.

"Look!" shouted someone in the crowd.

"It's him!" shouted someone else.

Instantly the outsiders' attention focused on Walter and Sancho. Floodlights and camera flashes blinded them with a concussion of white glare.

"It's Walter Parks," added someone helpfully in case anyone in the crowd hadn't actually figured this out for themselves.

"And some... guy," shouted someone perhaps thinking there might be blind people present.

Walter spotted his neighbour Steve. Steve, who had been vociferously shouting his opinions at the Sheriff, now turned and begun pointing and shouting inaudible suggestions at anyone else who would listen.

At that moment, one police officer suddenly remembered he was armed, drew his gun and opened fire. Not wanting to be left out, his fellow officers also drew their weapons and began shooting with wild abandon.

Walter and Sancho ducked below the barricade as the barrage of bullets battered the building blocks.

"Oh my," said Walter, no longer at all sure of his circumstances, "Oh my..."

* * *

Sheila walked backwards as she addressed the camera. She was making her way towards a press conference that the Sheriff was holding, while continuing her live update on the situation. "...where Plansville resident Walter Parks has decided to simply say 'no' to foreclosure. We're going to hear now from the Sheriff, who was personally first on the scene and is currently in charge of diffusing the situation."

All of the many times she had spent practicing her "concerned facial expressions" in the mirror at home went out the window. Knowing that she was live, simply holding the mic and forming the words took every ounce of her concentration. Walking backwards only added to the pressure. She'd made Bob, the cameraman, promise to warn her if she were about to trip or walk into someone, but she wasn't entirely sure she could trust him. She reached the gathered throng of reporters and gestured to Bob to focus on the Sheriff.

The Sheriff was also nervous at the idea of doing something stupid on national television. This is worse than YouTube, he thought. His nervousness evidenced itself in the form of peevishness. He'd been told in police executive training to imagine reporters were something less threatening, but nothing came to mind. The Sheriff wondered which microphone to address. "As many of you already know, what we're dealing with here is a common enough situation of a resisted foreclosure. The situation, however, has been made more complicated as a result of the rather formidable barriers erected by the resident in question. We are aware of four people inside of the house, Walter Parks, his wife Dawn Parks, and their infant daughter Hope Parks. There is also a Mexican-American man named Sancho whose relationship to the Parks is currently unknown."

One of the reporters waved his hand and asked, "Any truth to the rumour that the Parks family are hostages of this Sancho?"

"No, as far as we are aware, Mr. Panza is a friend and, or, possible victim of Mr. Parks."

More reporters waved their hands. They look like monkeys, thought the Sheriff. They look like funny monkey's waving their hands. He relaxed and imagined the microphones were bananas. He pointed to one of the monkeys.

"Eep?" said the monkey. "Eep, eep, eep?"

The Sheriff shook his head, "I'm sorry can you repeat that?"

"Is it true that he's an illegal immigrant?" asked the monkey who was now a reporter once more.

"No, we believe Walter Parks is a US Citizen," said the Sheriff. One of the Sheriff's deputies leaned forward and whispered into his ear. "Oh... oh right," said the Sheriff. He then addressed the microphones once more, "Um, so, if this Sancho is here illegally, he will first be rescued and then deported."

"Sheriff!" shouted another reporter with bushy red hair. He looks more like an orangutang, thought the Sheriff. Unsure whether he wanted to take a question from an orangutang, the Sheriff pointed to Sheila who had only discretely raised her hand. He didn't remember her name, but he knew her as the attractive local reporter from police fundraising events. He knew her and liked her.

"Sheriff, any comment on rumours that, because of your department's inexperience with anything like this, the FBI may take over the operation?"

The Sheriff wasn't so certain he liked Sheila anymore. He held up his hands for attention and addressed her directly, "Let me just say this... the Plansville Police Department is the finest in the world and have the situation completely under control. As you can see, we have the house fully surrounded. I think it's safe to say, Mr. Parks and his family *aren't going anywhere.*"

He emphasized this last sentence firmly. That should do it, he thought.

"But isn't that exactly what they want?" Sheila asked.

The Sheriff opened his mouth to respond sharply then, having no good answer, stopped and closed it. He considered what to say, opened his mouth again, then reconsidered and closed it again. Flashbulbs flashed, and cameras clicked. He had to say something. He turned to the other reporters and asked, "Next question?"

Instantly the reporters began to shout and wave their hands. The problem with monkeys, the Sheriff realized, was it's only a matter of time before they start throwing poop at you.

* * *

The Sheriff entered the operations van and took a fizzing plastic cup of Alka Seltzer from Officer Daniels. He downed the contents in a single gulp, almost choking on the half-dissolved disc. "Who the hell is that woman?"

"A reporter from Channel 8," Daniels answered, taking back the empty cup.

"I know that! What's her name?"

"Sheila Blitz."

"Uh huh," said the Sheriff. "That's a stupid name."

"Yes, sir."

The van was a large modified camper van. At a cost of one million dollars, the interior had been gutted and refitted with desks, computers, phones, satellite internet and more. They had originally intended to outfit the exterior with bulletproof siding, but that turned out to be a simple add-on for vehicles sold in Texas, so they'd ordered from there. The Sheriff had petitioned for years to get a mobile operations van and for years the damn liberals in government had opposed the idea. Finally, the political pendulum had swung and common sense was back in town. The Plansville PD now had more officers, a riot squad, gas masks, wiretap equipment nobody knew how to use yet and, of course, the van. The Sheriff peered out the bulletproof one-way glass window at the Parks castle walls and thought, somedays it's good to be *the man*.

"Damn buzzards. All they want is a piece of me. Now, I know how Dick Cheney felt."

"Yes, sir," said Daniels, who now handed him his coffee.

"It's all analysis and criticism. Never 'good job' or 'thanks for sticking your neck out', you know? "

"Yes, sir, I know."

The van was packed with officers monitoring phones, TVs and computer screens. We shoulda got the Empress model, thought the Sheriff, I knew the Princess was too small. He glanced down the line of computer monitors; two were stuck on blue screens while a third was installing Windows updates. "What the hell is going on here?" he demanded.

The various officers looked up at him in surprise.

Before anyone could answer, one of the female officers waved frantically at him from the back, "Sir!"

"What is it..." The Sheriff tried to remember her name, Howwits... Hoddits...? All he could think of was what the men called her, "Hot Tits", but he was pretty sure that wasn't her real name. "...you?"

"Sir, we have Parks on the line."

"Walter Parks?"

"Yes, sir."

"Damn. My office!" The Sheriff handed his coffee back to Daniels and plowed through the narrow passageway towards the back of the van. "This is it, people, this is it!"

* * *

The Sheriff's office was a mess. He'd wanted his office to feel like home and had brought some of his wife's collection of Franklin Mint Presidential plates to decorate. This had worked fine so long as the van had remained parked inside the police lot. The drive over, however, had not been kind to the porcelain Presidents. The Sheriff stepped on the remains of James K. Polk with an audible crunch as he made his way around to the other side of his desk.

He waved for Daniels to close the door as he dug through his files for the document he needed. He finally found a small booklet and laid it down on the desk. The title reassuringly read in a large friendly font, *So you need to negotiate a Hostage Situation...*

He opened the booklet to page one, the *Quick Start Guide*. He had no time to read through the various introductory paragraphs and warnings. He'd meant to do that before, of course, and had even started to once, but had fallen asleep as he always did when reading in bed. He waved to Daniels who handed him the phone extension, cleared his throat, and said, "Sheriff Thompson here."

"Hello," said Walter.

"Yes, hello," said the Sheriff, buying time as he scanned the page for a place to start. Fortunately, the guide had broken down the negotiation process into clearly marked steps. The book's authour had actually written several *For Dummies* books and had applied lessons learned here. The margins included helpful icons. For example *Don'ts* were marked with a picture of a bullet-riddled body in the margin.

The Sheriff's finger traced the first step.

1. Establish rapport with the suspect.

"How are you?" asked the Sheriff.

"I'm... fine?" said Walter, thrown off by this unexpected chitchat. Not wanting to appear impolite, he asked, "How about yourself?"

"Very well, thank you" said the Sheriff. Not sure that this was enough yet to establish rapport he then asked, "Do you like sports?"

"Not especially."

"Oh," said the Sheriff. He didn't know what to say about that but decided he could move on to step 2.

2. Learn the suspect's demands.

"So, Mr. Parks... May I call you Walter?"

"Sure."

"So, Walter, what are your demands?"

There was a pause before Walter responded, "Um... I haven't got any."

"You haven't got any?"

"Well, I want to be left alone I suppose, but I don't think that's what you mean."

"No, I suppose not," the Sheriff admitted. He read ahead to the next step, hoping to find out that step 2 was a formality.

3. Play for time. Feign effort to meet the suspects demands, lead them on until they break.

A cold flood of panic washed through the Sheriff's body. The words "Feign effort to meet the suspects demands..." pulsed in his head like a neon sign in a Dunkin' Donuts window. He covered the receiver with his hand and whispered to Officer Daniels, "The next step is about stringing him along and playing out his demands."

"So, what are his demands?" asked Daniels.

"He hasn't got any!" hissed the Sheriff.

"Oh."

"Hello?" said Walter.

The Sheriff racked his brain for answers and secretly swore at the little booklet. The Amazon.com description had guaranteed it would "help resolve any hostage situation". He made a mental note to go online later and give the book zero stars and a stinging review. For now, he would have to fly solo. "Yes, hello, Walter. Um... you're sure we can't interest you in a big duffle bag of money?"

"No, thank you," said Walter.

"Perhaps an escape helicopter?"

"I don't want to escape."

The Sheriff was truly flustered now. He forced himself to sound calm and, with mechanical deliberation, said, "Can I call you back?"

"Okay."

The Sheriff placed the receiver down gingerly, as if it were a venomous snake which had fallen asleep in his hand. His training had prepared him for any number of responses from criminals, ranging from cool calculation to outright aggression. Casual indifference, however, was not among the prepared profiles. It was as if Walter himself were as surprised as anyone to be here right now. The Sheriff threw up his hands in frustration, "He's being completely unreasonable. If he has no demands then we can't very well meet them, can we?"

"We would meet his demands?" asked Daniels incredulously.

"No, no, of course not, but... this is not how it's supposed to work!"

"Oh."

"He makes his demands. We pretend to consider them, maybe send in some pizza. Lots of back and fourth, yadda yadda yadda and bam! It's over."

"Just like that?

"Exactly like that."

"So what now?"

"Now?" the Sheriff considered. "Now, we go to plan B"

"Plan B? What the heck is Plan B?"

CHAPTER 10

"I'm just going to take a little off the top" - J. Guillotine

Walter and Dawn sat in the living room. Dawn, as always, sat with the baby monitor on her lap ready to pounce at the slightest sound of concern. Walter had persuaded her to leave Hope's room only on the condition that Dawn could carry it everywhere. Her pretty face showed the scars of stress, dark circles under her eyes and a sallow taint in her already pale complexion.

Walter sat with the phone on his lap. He had just finished relating the conversation with the Sheriff to Dawn when Sancho entered the room. He and Sancho were taking turns patrolling the grounds. Later they would take sleeping shifts. For now, however, neither was tired. Taking on the world was both terrifying and rather invigorating at the same time. Sancho had compared the feeling to when he was a child at a friend's birthday. There had been a piñata and it had been his turn to swing at it blindfolded. "When the grownups finally pulled the mask from my eyes, I found that in my enthusiasm I had missed the target completely but knocked out two of the other children and given a black eye to one of the adults. I was not a violent boy, but the injured children were brothers who were both bullies, and the adult was their horrible father. It felt very oddly wonderful."

"Is all okay?" asked Sancho seeing the look on Walter's face.

"They think I'm a common criminal who's holding you guys against your will."

"But you're not!" said Dawn.

"I'm just telling you what they think."

"Well, tell them they're wrong."

"Yes," agreed Sancho, "We tell them!"

"Tell who exactly?"

Dawn considered this for a moment. "Well, it should be someone with stature, an elder statesman of some kind. Someone who people trust."

* * *

Larry King sat across from his guest in his traditional striped shirt, suspenders and tie. As always, he hunched over his microphone like a bigheaded bird of prey. His guest today was the actor Pierce Brosnan. Pierce, a British born actor most famous for playing James Bond in four of the movies, casually sat wearing his customary suit, tie and slightly raised eyebrow.

On the TV monitors a picture-in-picture shot in the bottom right showed a live aerial view of the 'Parks Family Home in Plansville, New Jersey'.

"That is quite a scene coming to us live from Plansville, New Jersey," said Larry. "I'm sitting here with my guest, actor Pierce Brosnan. What do you think Pierce?"

Pierce tried to decide if this was an opportunity to mention his forthcoming film role as an isosceles triangle in a live-action 3D adaptation of Edwin Abbot's *Flatland*. Not seeing any immediate relevancy, he decided to start talking and wait for an opportunity to present itself. "Well, of course, these are tough times for a lot of folks," he said. "I know many people in Hollywood who are looking for work these days, but that's no reason to take your family hostage."

"A very good point. And we will be joined shortly by CNN's hostage situation expert, who will walk us through exactly how police can diffuse this —" Larry stopped in mid-sentence, interrupted by an urgent buzz from his ear-piece. He held up his hand as he listened to the tinny voice of his producer, then turned directly to the camera, "Oh wow, I am just receiving word that we have Walter Parks himself on the line. We have verified to the best of our knowledge that this is the real Walter Parks and..." Larry paused again to listen, then continued, "Okay, put him through."

"Hello Larry?" said Walter from the studio speakerphone.

"Yes, hello Walter, you're on the air."

Pierce was getting concerned about how this could all relate back to *Flatland*. He had been initially hesitant about even taking the role, but when he found out that the director was Stephen Spielberg he'd jumped.

Spielberg told him that he had immediately thought of Pierce to portray the two-dimensional character. Now, however, as he mulled this over, Pierce wasn't entirely sure it had been a compliment. Still, the script was very good with all sorts of jokes about "having a point" and "going off on a tangent" and everyone agreed the musical number 'I'm a Love Triangle' sung by Tom Jones was destined for number one.

"Thank you," said Walter. "I'd like to respond to something you and lot of news stations have been reporting about this being a 'hostage situation'."

"Okay, go ahead."

"Well, it's just... this is my house, my wife is here by choice and we're both the legal guardians of our child, for whom we only want the best. The only other person here is our contractor Sancho, who is also here by choice."

"Is true!" shouted Sancho in the background enthusiastically.

"So," Walter continued, "since none of us are being held against our will... well, I just don't think you can have a hostage situation without any hostages."

"He makes a good point there, Larry," agreed Pierce, with his natural suavity.

Larry nodded, then paused a moment to listen to his earpiece. He then explained, "It looks like Walter has gone. Okay, so I understand we're going back live to the scene in Plansville, New Jersey, where police are gathering in sizable numbers, apparently ready to charge and scale the walls of the so-called 'castle'."

On the TV monitors the live feed from New Jersey in the bottom right zoomed up to fill the screen with an aerial view of the scene, where a phalanx of police in riot gear now gathered on Dream Street facing the castle walls.

* * *

Walter and Sancho crouched on the wall-walk behind the battlements, out of sight of the crowds and police outside. Walter pocketed his cellphone and peered between the concrete blocks that formed the walls' tooth-like crenellations. He was amazed they had made it up here unseen by the helicopters overhead, but all seemed focused on the forces gathering below. Walter understood their fascination; he too now watched with trepidation as the battalion of police formed into a unified mass of plexiglass shields, helmets and nightsticks. For a moment, the mass glowed with blue lightening as tasers were tested for effectiveness. One officer, inadvertently tased by his fellow, was carried away, smoking, to the infirmary tent to recover.

The spectacle had allowed Walter and Sancho to drag into position the heavy object that now sat between them.

"You ready?" asked Walter.

"Si," said Sancho.

* * *

The Sheriff walked down the line of men in riot gear like a general inspecting his troops or, in his mind, like an NFL football coach before the big game.

"All right men, the whole world is watching. This is our chance to show that we can shut this down and shut it down fast."

"Yes, sir!" the men shouted back in unison. They'd practiced this shouting for months for just such an occasion as this. The problem had been Caruthers with his damn high pitch choirboy voice. Finally, the Sheriff had to tell him to shut-the-hell-up and just mouth the words. It had worked beautifully. All of that practice made them sound like a well oiled machine. He listened as the crowd gave a gratifying gasp of excitement. This is it, he thought, the Superbowl.

"And to think they said we'd never need riot gear in Plansville," the Sheriff smirked, "Who's laughing now?"

"You sir!" shouted the men in unison.

"Damn straight." The Sheriff stepped back to face them all. I should have brought a horse, he thought, imagining himself mounted high with his arms raised like General Patton before the Battle of the Bulge. He then realized he didn't actually know how to ride a horse and the image in his mind changed to that of himself being dragged through the crowd by his feet caught in the stirrups. Perhaps just as well, he decided. With his feet firmly planted on terra firma, the Sheriff raised his arms and cleared his throat. "Now then, on the count of three. One... two... three!"

The men surged forward, batons banging fiercely on shields. Suddenly, the Sheriff realized he was an extremely movable object directly in the path of that unstoppable force. He exchanged stares with the first line of equally surprised officers who had just arrived at the same conclusion. Pressed forward by those behind, they continued their march towards him. The Sheriff was forced to lift his arms straight up into the air and pirouette between two of the columns, desperately dancing to avoid being swept along in the onslaught.

After this initial slip up, the first phase of the plan went exactly as ordered. A whistle blew, and the police halted at the edge of the moat. Plywood boards were passed up the ranks and laid down over the water forming instant bridges to the other side.

The Sheriff who had taken the opportunity to wend his way out of the formation, once more smiled with satisfaction as impressed murmurs traversed the crowd. Exactly as I drew it on the blackboard, he thought. He imagined being interviewed by Sean Hannity who would introduce him as 'the brilliant strategist who had defeated anarchist Walter Parks'. He would then explain to Sean the difference between strategy and tactics; he'd always wanted to do that on television. First down, he thought.

As the first row of men crossed the moat successfully, the subsequent rows passed forward their next secret weapon, ladders. This too went exactly as they'd rehearsed it. Hand over hand the aluminum ladders were pushed into position and thrown against the castle walls.

Second down, thought the Sheriff, maybe third and fourth too. What the hell, he decided, *touchdown*.

At that moment the Sheriff heard a familiar voice. It was Walter Parks's voice yelling "Now!" That didn't sound plaintive or capitulary, the Sheriff thought with surprise.

Walter and Sancho appeared from behind the castle battlements, heaving a large object into view. Despite the night, the dozens of floodlights and news cameras focused on the walls highlighted every detail with near blinding daylight from every direction. The Sheriff studied the unusual object, and one compound noun formed in his surprised brain, "water cannon". Water cannon? He thought, that wasn't part of the plan.

A pillar of white water erupted from the cannon nozzle and struck full on the front line of officers, sending shields flying from padded gloves.

"Where the hell'd they get a water cannon?" the Sheriff shouted indignantly, "That's our thing!"

The torrential blast sent the men sliding backwards into the water as the moat banks turned instantly to mud. The precarious plywood bridges tilted and flipped sending more men splashing into the water below.

"Retreat!" shouted Officer Caruthers in a girlish squeal.

"Retreat!" the rest agreed in disjointed harmony.

The officers scrambled backwards out of the moat, crawling up the outer banks and over one another trying to escape the pounding pressure of the cannon's blast.

The Sheriff opened his mouth to cry foul or at least demand a timeout when the column of water struck him clear in the chest, sending him hurtling backwards.

"We won! We won!" shouted Walter and Sancho in unison.

The crowd, ever fickle with their affection, gasped with approval at the defenders' apparent victory.

Other police officers who had not partaken in the failed raid opened fire, forcing Walter and Sancho to duck below the parapets once more.

As the battery of bullets continued, Sancho and Walter exchanged a low five. The exuberant rush of adrenaline and flush of victory overcame any feelings of fear.

"You the king, Walter!" Sancho shouted. "You the king!"

Walter smiled and nodded his head in acknowledgment of the accolade.

"You the Lord of all you survey, man" added Sancho with a smile.

Yes, I am, thought Walter as he looked across his fortified lawn, I do believe I am.

CHAPTER 11

"I can see my house from here." - N. Armstrong

The Channel 8 camera panned past a dejected line of sopping wet policemen. Some dumped water from their helmets while others attempted to wring out their uniforms while still wearing them. They squinted at the camera lights and appeared stunned and confused by the outcome of the attack. The Sheriff glowered at the lens and stomped away. "With the first attempt to storm the castle over," said Sheila, in a voiceover, "it's easy to see in this round who the losers are."

"Hey!" protested one of the dripping officers.

The camera panned away before coming to rest on Sheila Blitz who smiled and said into the microphone, "So now let's find out what the ever growing crowd of neighbours and curious onlookers has to say about the siege taking place in their own backyard."

Sheila turned to the crowd of gawkers who pressed against the police barricades. Most had been there for hours, dressed in warm coats and hats to withstand the night temperatures. Now, invigorated by the recent battle and excited by the prospect of being on TV, they waved and aped for the camera. Sheila had already picked her mark, an angry looking red-haired man who had cheered the police assault and cursed their defeat. "What do you think of the siege, sir?" she asked him and held the microphone out for his response.

"God damn it," he snarled, "I think they should just torch the place. You know, napalm them out? That'd fix 'em."

"I see," said Sheila. "But wouldn't that defeat the purpose of repossessing the house?"

"Yeah, well, whatever. It'd also teach winey snots like Parks how the real world works. Goddamn welfare bum!"

Sheila gave a practiced nod. It was the kind of nod that every reporter needs to master. The nod that says, I acknowledge what you say without actually agreeing with it. This nod was especially important when dealing with angry people. Angry people made good TV programs that viewers wanted to watch. Rational people made for, well, PBS. "Thank you sir," she added. Before he could launch into some sort of tirade, she moved her mic over to another onlooker. This man was short and wore small round 'John Lennon' glasses that reflected the illuminated castle walls behind. "And what do you think, sir?" Sheila asked.

"Well, I think Walter Parks is a hero," he said with a proud smile. "I think he's standing up for every American who struggles just to keep it all together. Most of us are just a few bad breaks away from being Walter

Parks."

The angry onlooker shouted from off camera, "Yeah? Well, how'd you like a few bad breaks, ya pansy?"

"Thank you, sir," said Sheila. Deciding it best not to exasperate the situation, she turned and walked away from the crowd. "And there we have it..." she began.

Behind her the argument continued. "I'm allowed to have my own opinion," said the smaller man.

"Not if it's a wussy opinion."

"...a mix of views in attendance," Sheila continued, "some in support of Walter Parks and some opposed to him. But what about those who know Walter—his family, friends or neighbours?"

On queue, Bob the cameraman panned slightly to bring Steve Prefect into frame. Behind them the bespectacled man sternly waggled a finger at the angry red-haired man. The angry man responded by moving his hands in a way that indicated he would like to make freshly squeezed orange juice with the other man's head.

"So let's speak to one of Walter Parks's immediate neighbours, Mr. Steven Prefect." She paused while Steve gave a serious smile to the camera. "Mr. Prefect, did you ever suspect that your neighbour might be capable of this sort of action?"

"Absolutely," said Steve. "A freakin' ticking time-bomb waiting to go off. Most people probably didn't see it, but I did."

At this point, behind them, the angry man lunged through the intervening crowd members at the smaller man. The smaller man shrieked and attempted to retreat only to find his way blocked by the tightly packed bodies of other onlookers.

"So why not warn Police if you knew he was dangerous?" asked Sheila.

Members of the crowd attempted to restrain the angry man.

"Well..." said Steve, "technically, I couldn't prove it. But let me tell you something Sheila, as someone who has made his money the old fashioned way, by honest, hard work as an investment banker, I agree with many people in this crowd. I am disgusted by takers like Walter Parks. He messed up his life, so now he needs to pay the consequences."

At that moment, the angry onlooker broke free of his fellows and landed on the smaller man. Both disappeared below camera level save for the occasional fist and flying footwear.

Steve turned and, pointing his finger directly at the camera like the archetypal Uncle Sam, said, "Walter, if you're watching right now, grow up. Just grow-the-hell-up."

Sheila tilted the microphone back to herself and concluded, "And there we have it. This is Sheila Blitz reporting. Ted, back to you."

She held her pose for a moment until Bob dropped his hand and said, "And we're out."

"Are we done?" asked Steve.

"We're done. Thank you, Mr. Prefect."

Steve nodded with satisfaction and walked away.

"Was that okay?" Sheila asked Bob.

"Absolutely, Miss Nationwide Coverage," said Bob with a smile. Bob's usual sardonic wit had evaporated since they had first discovered the castle. His 'nothing ever happens here' cynicism had been replaced by a somehow more disturbing 'isn't this exciting?' sincerity.

"What?" said Sheila.

"We're being picked up by the ABC and CNN... This is the big time, baby, the big time."

But they're all here... that's a CNN helicopter up there!"

"Apparently they like the local touch," shrugged Bob. "Apparently, you keep it real."

"Oh," said Sheila as the implications of this sank in, "That's right. I do. I do keep it real."

* * *

Hope's room was dark. Dawn, her eyes long adjusted to the dim ambient light, stood over the crib watching her baby sleep. She wondered, as she so often had, at the infant's tiny nose, cherubic cheeks and small chest rising and falling with each breath. In and out... in and out... in and out...

With a roar of heavenly furor, a news helicopter passed overhead. Briefly the floodlight from its undercarriage overwhelmed the window drapes and filled the room with blinding white brilliance. Then, it was gone and darkness returned.

Hope stirred in her sleep.

Walter passed the bedroom door then, realizing Dawn was there, backed up and entered. He looked at Hope, then at his wife. "How is she?" he asked.

"She'd be better without those damn helicopters."

Walter nodded, and both watched in silence as Hope settled again. Walter realized it was the first time he'd heard Dawn say the word 'damn'.

"You know," he began, "if I'd guessed things would blow up like this... I just thought..." Dawn looked at him. Her gaze flooded him with awareness of the stupidity of anything he might say about their circumstances. "I don't know what I thought."

"It's okay," she said, with that impossible charity that was Dawn, "You're just keeping your promise." She held up something that Walter took a moment to recognize in the shadow. It was Hope's baby book. Dawn opened it to the page that read, 'Baby's 1st Birthday'. The page was otherwise, expectantly blank. "In all the craziness, we forgot. It's in just one week."

Walter took her in his arms, held her close and kissed her deeply. The helicopter passed once more and, for a moment, they were all three silhouettes in its supernova glare.

CHAPTER 12

"All of our stereo types are unique." - Masaru Ibuka

The scratchy call of the Western Scrub Jay sounded in Walter and Dawn's bedroom that morning. The Western Scrub Jay, as the name implied, was not commonly found in New Jersey, especially inside people's houses. It was followed by the call of the Jamaican White Eyed Vireo and the Mexican Jay. All of this was accompanied by the gentle trickle of brook water.

The rising sun sent a bright yellow beam between a gap in the curtains and poked Walter directly in the face. Walter, still asleep, scrunched his nose and shifted out of the sunbeam's reach. A gentle breeze lifted the curtain and allowed the sunbeam to jab to the left, smacking Walter upside the head with morning brightness. Walter, dazed by the attack, opened his eyes and looked about the bedroom in a perplexed bleary-eyed stupor. No Dawn, registered his brain's neurons, still flickering into consciousness like old fluorescent light bulbs. She must be making breakfast, he concluded.

Walter slid out of bed and silenced the sleep sounds machine in mid-warble. He then pulled on his robe and slippers and shuffled to the window. Bracing himself for the blast of sunshine, he flung the curtains wide. After a series of blinks, his eyes adjusted to the panoramic scene of police cars, news crews, and huddled masses of onlookers encircling his home.

"Oh... right," he said.

* * *

The rising sun was also having its effects out on Dream Street. Of course, a shift of police and news media had been awake all night. There had even been rumours of a nighttime raid but the disaffected, humiliated force had been unable to muster the manpower for such an assault. The Sheriff had not planned to fail in the initial attempt and the irregular patrols of Sancho along the castle walls showed that they were prepared for any such actions.

Now, as the warm sunbeams crossed the crowds, arms were stretched, dew was wiped from groundsheets and a contingent of entrepreneurs arrived reselling Starbucks coffee and McDonalds Egg McMuffins.

Steve Prefect, still in bathrobe, opened his front door to pick up his morning paper. Not finding it on his welcome mat, he looked up to see that there was now a police car parked on his front lawn. There was also a group of teenagers in sleeping bags and a large British bulldog. The bulldog, which bore the same slight resemblance to Winston Churchill that all bulldogs do, eyed him with indifference. All of the teenagers were asleep save one who lay propped on elbows, reading Steve's Wall Street Journal.

"Hey, get the hell off my lawn!" yelled Steve.

"Chill out dude," said the teenager, turning to an article on the overheated foreign exchange market. The other teenagers began to stir and groan.

"No, you chill out!"

"I am chilled out."

Steve tried to think of an angry retort, but the best he could come up with was to roar with furry and storm at them. "Ahhh!" he yelled.

"Man, it is too early for this," moaned one of awakening teens.

"Ahhh!" Steve reiterated.

"Christ, we're going!" said the first teenager.

They slowly gathered up their sleeping bags.

"Ahhh!" shouted Steve, once more to encourage them. By this time Steve had turned beet red and the vein in his forehead had begun to dance the samba.

"You really should get that looked at," said one teen as he hooked a leash onto the bulldog's collar. The dog looked up at Steve with somber, heavy lidded eyes. "A man does what he must — in spite of personal consequences, in spite of obstacles and dangers and pressures, and *that* is the basis of all human morality," the dog seemed to say.

"Ahhh!" shouted Steve, waving his arms for emphasis. The group of young men began to shuffle to the street. "Not that!" Steve snarled, pointing to the newspaper still in the first youth's hands.

"Whatever," shrugged the teen, and he dropped the paper to the grass.

"And don't come back!" shouted Steve at the teens as they walked away. Several gave him the finger over their shoulders. "Punks! Goddamn punks!"

Steve shook his head, picked up the dropped paper, turned and stepped directly into the dog poop deposited by the teens' bulldog the night before.

* * *

Bob had never planned on being a local television news cameraman. His goal had been to be a feature film director or, failing that, a pornographic film director. Shooting for Channel 8 was only supposed to have been a stepping stone on his path to greatness, or copious amounts of nudity, as the case may be. He'd briefly worked as a cameraman for MTV, on a show that interviewed musical performers. There, he had been required to continually jump around to keep the camera moving on whomever the talking head might be. The idea was to effectively fidget for the ADD afflicted audience and, at the same time, make John Mayer or whomever it was, appear far more interesting than they actually were. Bob had left the exhausting post after suffering an epileptic fit in the editing room and had come home to Plansville and Channel 8 news. Being a news cameraman required exactly two skills, point and shoot, Bob ruminated bitterly as he sipped on his exorbitantly priced resold Starbucks Grandé Coffee. He had purchased the coffee for only ten dollars from a highly unreasonable Mexican named Julio. After five minutes of negotiations, Julio had thrown in the packets of sugar "for free". In return, Bob had let Julio call him a 'stupid caffeine addicted gringo'. Still, the coffee tasted good.

Some distance in front of Bob stood the Sheriff and a half-dozen of his men staring blankly at the castle walls, oblivious to Bob's presence. On the hood of the police cruiser between them sat an open box of Dunkin' Donuts and an empty coffee tray. Bob watched in fascination as they all together, with unconscious synchronicity, dipped their doughnuts in their coffees, took a bite and wiped their chins. He had heard that women who spent a lot of time together synchronize their monthly cycles. Perhaps this was the same thing? Dip, bite, wipe... Dip, bite, wipe... Feeling the tug of his Director's dream or at least the opportunity of a YouTube video, Bob lifted the camera and pressed record. Dip, bite, wipe...

"I want to talk to you," demanded Steve.

The Sheriff started from his daze "Aw Hell," he moaned.

"How long are you going to let this go on? Look at the mess on my lawn. Look at it!" Steve gestured at the parked police car and trampled grass. "You are letting this man make a mockery of American values!"

The Sheriff popped the last piece of his doughnut into his mouth and reached for another. "And what is it exactly you propose we do, Mr. Prefect?"

"You have helicopters, just shoot him! Shoot Walter Parks in the head!"

The Sheriff shook his head bemusedly, as did many of the other officers. "And how do you think that would look on television?"

"Who cares? He's assaulted your men."

"With water cannons. I have been clearly instructed not to use lethal force unless he does. It's not... popular."

Steve through up his hands and shouted, "So that's what this is about? Politics?"

The Sheriff shrugged, "Ain't everything?"

"No!" said Steve with earnest surprise, "Usually it's about money."

The Sheriff took a bite of his doughnut, which immediately squirted yellow ooze down his shirt. "Damnation," he swore. "Goddamn Boston cream." He looked about for a napkin and spotted a convoy of black sedan cars making their way through the crowd. "Aw double Hell. Here they come, the Federal Bureau of Emasculation."

The Ford sedans pulled to a stop directly in front of the Sheriff and his men. The doors of the lead car opened, and two agents in plain black business suits exited. The first was a tall Pakistani-American. The second was a short Jewish man who, as a strict follower of the Talmud, also wore a Yarmulka and full beard. The Sheriff, despite his anger, couldn't help but note the changing face of the FBI. Damn affirmative action, he rued. "So you're the guys come to chop off my dick?"

"Yes, sir," said the Pakistani agent matter-of-factly, "I'm Agent Rashid Rajput and this Agent Joshua Weisz."

"Hello there," said Agent Weisz, waving cheerfully.

"We're now officially commandeering this operation. As the head of local law enforcement you and your men and are welcome to observe and assist."

The Sheriff rolled his eyes, "The more things change the more things stay the same."

"I'm sorry?"

"Well, you don't look like your classic G-Men, but you sure do act like 'em."

There was a moment of awkward silence. The Sheriff wondered if he'd crossed a line he'd regret. Finally, Agent's Weisz's eyes lit up, "I believe he means the updated standard issue suits."

"Ah yes, the wider lapels," nodded Agent Rajput in understanding.

"Yeah," said the Sheriff, "that's exactly what I meant."

* * *

Walter and Sancho watched this exchange between the Sheriff and the new arrivals from the parapets. He and Sancho had been taking Jesus around the wall-walk, getting the dog exercise and scoping out the enemy positions at the same time. Jesus had finally stopped barking at the outsiders and focused instead on what really mattered, the distant smell of Dunkin' Donuts.

"Who are they?" wondered Walter.

"A rabbit and a convenience store owner?" said Sancho.

"What?"

"Sorry, rabbi. A rabbi and a convenience story owner."

"Why would the Sheriff be talking to a convenience store owner?"

"Perhaps a software engineer?"

"How can you say that? No, they're clearly authorities of some kind. They're wearing suits."

"Rabbi's wear suits."

"And non-Rabbi's wear Yarmulkas"

"Hmmm..." said Sancho, unconvinced.

"You can't stereotype people like that!"

"Why not?"

"Because... well how would you like it people said you were a stereotype?"

"But I'm not."

Walter opened his mouth to argue, but decided to let it go. Sancho had been the best ally he could ever hope for. The man had stuck with him out of principle and the last thing he wanted to do was drive a rift between them.

Sancho looked about at the dozens of police, media and thousands of onlookers all focused on them. He patted down his hair and sucked in his gut. "You're sure they won't shoot us anymore?" he asked.

"The governor himself said so on TV. Apparently I've become 'too popular'."

"You?"

"And you, by extension."

"Oh," Sancho considered this, then smiled and said, "Maybe we win this after all. You think, sir?"

"Sancho, you need to stop calling me 'sir'. I'm not your superior. You're doing me a tremendous favour by being here."

Sancho shook his head in firm disagreement. "No, sir. This is the point. You are like those toys you have."

"Toys?" said Walter. "Oh my collectable figures, my knights."

"Exactly. You are a knight fighting for what is right, a champion for the people. So you are a 'sir', Sir Walter."

Walter stopped and stared at Sancho in surprise. Jesus took the opportunity to lift a leg at one of the castle wall's merlons. Walter didn't know what to say. He started to speak anyway, "Sancho, I..."

"You see?" shouted Sancho excitedly and pointed at Walter's chest. "You said it yourself... you are now bulletproof!"

Walter followed Sancho's finger to the red laser dot wavering slightly on his chest. He then looked up to see the corresponding laser sight sniper rifle aimed by a SWAT sharpshooter on Steve's rooftop. As if in a dream, Walter caught the laser dot on his palm.

The sniper did not flinch, nor adjust his position. He knew that, if the order came, the bullet would easily pass through Walter's hand, torso, and beyond. He watched as Walter's hand, zoomed large in the rifle's scope, turned to give him the finger. The sharpshooter was tempted to shoot off the finger tip but did not. He had his orders.

Walter's initial cold rush of fear turned to a warm rush of adrenaline. He was invincible. Sancho was right. He was a knight in shining armour.

Walter turned to his Mexican sidekick and smiled, "Sancho, there's something I want to show you."

* * *

Walter opened the access door to the garage with his heart pounding. He had never shown anyone other than Dawn, Hope and Jesus his little project and none of them understood it. Sancho entered behind him and Walter switched on the light.

The single bulb flickered to life, illuminating the two car space. Walter's green chevy cavalier was parked on one side. The other was filled entirely by an eight-foot high structure covered in black tarpaulin.

Walter gestured proudly at the mysterious shroud.

"Ah yes," said Sancho, "I see this thing while we worked on the walls. Olaf even peeked and says it is a picnic table you are working on."

Walter stared at him, deflated. "You peeked?"

"Olaf peeked. We needed tools."

"Oh. Well this is no picnic table, it's..." Walter dramatically swept back the tarp revealing the heavy wooden structure beneath. For the past two years Walter had been faithfully building a full-sized, fully operational medieval catapult. Massive wooden logs formed the frame, while thick ropes tied around spindles held down the spring-loaded firing arm.

Sancho stared at it in wonder, then finally said, "This does not look like a very comfortable picnic table."

"It's not a picnic table!" shouted Walter in exasperation, "It's a catapult."

"A cata-what?"

"A catapult. For..." Walter pointed to the heavy wooden bowl. "You put things in there." He then made a yanking motion. "Then pull the lever and... zing!" He drew the arc of an imaginary trajectory.

"Oh... una catapulta!"

Walter stared at him. "That's like the same word with an 'a' the end. How could you not..." He let it go. Sancho didn't seem nearly as impressed as Walter had expected him to be. His reaction made Walter doubt the dream he'd held for so long, plus it was annoying. "Anyway, I wanted to build a trebuchet, but this seemed easier."

"Trebu...?"

"Trebuchet? I think it's French." Walter made more gestures to mimic that particular weapon of war. He ended with flinging his arm

127

over his head while standing on one foot.

"Ah, I see," said Sancho with sudden comprehension.

"What do you call a trebuchet in Spanish?" asked Walter.

"A trebuchet," said Sancho.

Walter started to comment, but again decided to move on. "Yes, well, the problem is they're much taller so I would have had to cut a hole in the roof."

"Yes," said Sancho in agreement as if discussing the most sensible location for a sofa. He then began to walk around the catapult. Walter was gratified to see admiration finally begin to register on the Mexican's face.

"This very, very impressive, sir. You work on this a long time, si?"

"Years. Of course, it was just a hobby, I never thought I might actually need it."

Sancho looked up with delight, "So we use it on the policia?"

"No, no, someone could really get hurt. Maybe even us, since I'm pretty sure a catapult counts as 'lethal force'."

Sancho looked disappointed but acquiesced. "Still, is nice to know is here," he said.

CHAPTER 13

"All cows eat grass." - W.A. Mozart

By evening, the T-shirt vendors had arrived on Dream Street in force. Members of the crowd could buy shirts that read either "Walt of the Earth" or "No Free Parksing" depending upon their feelings for or against Walter Parks. More neutral options included, "I Survived the Siege." and "The world's gone to Hell and I'll I got was this lousy T-Shirt." All of the T-shirts came from the good folks at TrimCo, who also offered such classics as "Beer, it's not just for breakfast anymore" and, of course, the always popular, "I'm with Stupid".

Federal Bureau of Investigation agents Rajput and Weisz stood over a tablet PC, placed on the hood of a police cruiser, in thoughtful discussion. The display shone in the darkening twilight like a slice of daylight. On screen was an enhanced satellite view of their current location.

"Is that Google Earth?" asked the Sheriff leaning between the two agents. Rajput and Weisz looked at him with surprise.

"No, Google Earth is static," explained Agent Rajput with annoyance. "This is a live satellite feed of the current location. It costs us thirty-thousand dollars per minute."

"Wow," said the Sheriff. He then pointed excitedly at a fuzzy splotch on the screen. "Is that us?"

"Yes, that's us."

The Sheriff looked up at the sky and began waving his arms, "Woo-hoo! Hello! Hello there!" As he did this he glanced back at the screen, then stopped, disappointed. "How come I can't see me waving?"

"There's a three-minute delay."

"Oh. That sucks."

Agents Rajput sighed, "Indeed. Is there anything we can help you with Sheriff?"

"Well," said the Sheriff, remembering his original purpose and own indignation, "I was wantin' to see if you'd care to share your no doubt brilliant plan with me."

"Technically, Sheriff, we're not required to."

"Okay..."

"But the field manual does indicate we should, where possible, facilitate our relationship by making you feel like you've been consulted and win your hearts and minds."

"My hearts and..." said the Sheriff surprised at being talked to as if he weren't there. "Okay, well, I appreciate your honesty. Look, you can trust me to keep my mouth shut."

"Oh that won't be necessary!" laughed Rajput. Weisz also chuckled and shook his head. "Not in about... one minute." Agent Rajput pointed to a group of four FBI agents setting up a large stereo speaker system atop a ten-foot pole. The Sheriff noticed other similar sets of audio speakers now surrounding the castle, all facing inwards. "The plan is to play very, very loud music."

"Very loud music?" asked the Sheriff.

"Very," Agent Rajput gestured deferentially to Agent Weisz. The diminutive Jew, prior to joining the FBI, had worked as a DJ in the all-night, all-Jewish New York Rave Club, 'Tummel Spiel' and was considered the agency field authority on the science of audio assault.

"Very loud," affirmed Agent Weisz, pointing to the ear plugs in his ears. "It sounds meshugass, but it was very effective against Noriega in '89. Of course, then we used Megadeath, but since then we have found far more powerful weaponry."

With that, Agent Weisz raised his hand to signal an FBI agent who had been standing by, holding an iPod like some sort of detonator. The FBI agent pressed 'play'. The instantly recognizable voice of Cher singing *If I Could Turn Back Time* began blasting from each of the assembled speakers.

"Oh jeez!" shouted the Sheriff, quickly covering his ears. Despite his best efforts, Cher's voice seeped between his fingers like a mixture of tapioca and treacle.

All around, surprised onlookers and officers covered their ears or fled altogether. A handful of Cher fans in the crowd, however, began to dance and cheer. Sheila, whose nearby interview with another neighbour was cut short, simply ordered Bob the cameraman to film the crowd reactions. She noticed, with some surprise, that among the dancers was the angry onlooker she had interviewed earlier. He punched the air and sang in some sort of Karaoke craze.

"What the hell is this?" shouted the Sheriff over the music.

"Cher," said Agent Rajput with a smile. "She's absolutely lethal. Lets see how Mr. Parks and his family are doing after three straight days of this played over and over and over again. Hmm?"

Steve Prefect lurched out of his house behind them with his hands over his ears. "Oh dear God!" he cried. One of his front windows shattered behind him as if to underscore his agony.

The Sheriff stared about in shock at the chaos gripping the scene. The FBI apparently had not thought to issue earplugs to anyone other than their own people.

On the satellite screen between them, a tiny blurry image began waving its arms.

* * *

Sancho and Walter hurried to nail the blankets to the window. It was the second last window to cover in Hope's bedroom. The music was perceptively muffled.

"See? It's already quieter," said Walter, "When we're done she won't hear it at all."

Dawn nodded without looking up from Hope who was fast asleep in her arms. "It actually seems to soothe her anyway," she said.

"Good, it's just as well. We may all have to sleep here to escape... that."

Sancho who was stapling in the edges of the blanket on his side began to bob his head and sing along, "...If I could da da da a way, I'd da da da–"

He stopped as he realized both Walter and Dawn were staring at him. "Sorry. It is very catchy..."

Jesus began to howl.

"Don't you start!" Walter reprimanded the dog, who whimpered in protest but quieted none-the-less. Satisfied, Walter drove in the last nail. He then picked up a blanket for the remaining window. "Okay help me with this one and we're done."

CHAPTER 14

"Be kind to a friend." - M. Nostredame

Sheila and Bob made their way across the street to where the two FBI agents stood waiting for them. It was night again and now "Day Three of the Siege", as they were calling it on TV. It was important to remember this. Lack of sleep, the daylight bright floodlights, and the continuously looping music, obliterated any sense of time or connection with reality. In this way it was exactly like being in a night club, a Las Vegas Casino or anywhere in Orange County, California.

Sheila paused as Bob raised the camera to his shoulder and trained it on her. He lifted his hand to count, three, two, one... The red 'live' light came on and Sheila began speaking into the mic while walking backwards towards the two agents. Bob followed. "We have been given the special privilege of following the FBI 'behind the scenes', as it were, to record this operation. It's all part of a new outreach campaign designed to give the bureau a more friendly face. We've agreed not to show any of this until after the matter has been resolved and to refer to the two agents with assumed cover names. Again, let me stress, these are not their real names."

By this point Sheila had reached agents Rajput and Weisz and turned to face them. "Hello Agent 'Johnson', Agent 'McTavish'."

"What?" shouted Agent Rajput-Johnson over the music.

"I said, hello!"

"I think she said hello," shouted Agent Weisz, aka McTavish.

Rajput removed his earplugs. "What?"

"Hello!" said Weisz.

"Why are you saying hello to me, Joshua? You've been here the whole time."

"Not me, her."

"Oh hello!" said Rajput turning to Sheila with a surprised smile. "Sheila, yes?"

"Yes," said Sheila. "Hello."

There was a moment of awkward silence before Sheila realized Rajput was waiting for her. "Perhaps, Agents 'Johnson' and 'McTavish', you could explain why you're keeping the whole neighbourhood awake with this music."

"Yes, we're sorry about that," answered Weisz, "but the music is all part of a carefully staged, multi-tier plan designed to resolve the situation quickly. I know it seems odd and perhaps even silly to a layperson such as yourself, but it has been used very successfully in the past. We know exactly what we're doing."

"Agent McTavish, wasn't this the same tactic used in Waco, Texas at the Branch Davidian complex siege in 1993?"

"Oh yes. Exactly so."

"But, Agent McTavish, many would say that was a complete disaster."

"Oy, well..." Weisz shrugged, "that depends on how you define 'success', my dear. You don't see many Branch Davidians around do you?"

"No, no, you do not."

At that moment a loud "KRACK!" sounded above the music as a gunshot struck one of the stereo speakers just feet away from them. The speaker shattered with a spray of sparks. Everyone dropped to the ground, and instantly dozens of guns were drawn and aimed at the castle walls, searching for a target.

"It's Parks!" shouted Rajput.

"Get down!" shouted Weisz to the few stunned onlookers who had continued to stand. Most dropped to the ground, while a few devoted dancers began to dance even harder.

More gunshots sounded, striking each speaker system one after another. Speaker cabinets spun and fell from their supports slowly silencing Cher. "If I could find a–" PTINNNNG!

Sheila directed Bob to train his camera on one of the remaining speakers. Sure enough, seconds later a bullet punctured the metal casing and sent the speaker crashing to the ground.

"That hit the back of the unit," Sheila shouted into the microphone. "That means the shots are not coming from inside the Parks's residence."

Many in the crowd of onlookers had also begun to realize that the bullets were not being aimed at them and rose slowly to their feet. The last speaker exploded, cutting off the chorus in mid-crescendo. For the first time in three days there was complete silence on Dream Street, no conversation, no gunfire, no Cher. The crowd burst into cheers and applause.

Agent Rajput, livid, jumped to his feet and pointed furiously at the shattered equipment. "Those speakers are property of the US Government, people. It is a federal offence to shoot them! Not good. Not good at all!"

The crowd paused a moment, then burst into even louder hoots and cheers.

* * *

With operation 'Diva Bomb' put on ice, at least until new sound equipment could be brought in, Agents Rajput and Weisz brought Sheila to witness the highly secret, primary operation underway. With the eager cooperation of its owner, they had set up an extensive base in Steve Prefect's backyard. This location had several advantages including being next door to the Parks's home and being away from the annoying crowd of onlookers. It also had a swimming pool, Jacuzzi and wet bar.

Sheila addressed the camera, microphone in hand, while Agent Rajput and Weisz staged a thoughtful discussion in the background. "Agents Johnson and McTavish have brought us to the backyard of neighbour Steve Prefect who has been very enthusiastic in his support of any effort to evict Walter Parks." Sheila turned and walked over to Rajput and Weisz. "Agents Johnson and McTavish, now that the audio weaponry has failed, can you tell us your next course of action?"

Rajput smiled and shook his head as if addressing a child. "The music is not a serious setback, because, as I explained, this is a multi-tier operation. A few moments ago, one of our agents went over this wall, here. Agent Weisz–"

"McTavish," Agent Weisz corrected him, then added "Arr..." for effect.

"Don't you mean 'ach'?" asked Sheila trying her best Scottish brogue. "'Arr' is what pirates say."

"Oh right... ach!" said Weisz, then shaking his head, "Oy."

"Anyway," continued Rajput. "Agent McTavish here is in direct contact with the agent."

Agent Weisz tapped a wire clipped to his ear to illustrate this.

"So," said Sheila with surprise, "you're saying that, as we speak, an FBI agent is infiltrating the Parks home?"

"That is exactly what I said. Well, not exactly, I used slightly different words, but yes."

"Does this Agent have a name?"

"He does. But, we can't tell you that. Let's call him Agent X."

* * *

Agent X crept stealthily across the Parks's lawn. He moved with the exacting precision of a black cat. Actually, he moved with the agility of a cat of any colour, had the cat any interest whatsoever in infiltrating the Parks's residence, which it likely would not have, given the presence of a rather large dog. That said, the operative was dressed in a black body stocking and mask which better explained the black cat comparison.

Agent X was the best stealth operative the agency had. Tapping into his ninja-like training, he carefully stepped between the individual blades of grass.

On the other side of the wall, Agent Rajput continued to explain the plan to Sheila with all the pride of an expectant father. "We chose this approach as the view from inside the house is blocked by the garage, so Parks won't be able to see him coming."

Agent X reached the side of the garage and paused to pull into place a pair of night vision goggles. Outside, the moonlight and ambient glow from beyond the wall had been sufficient to light his way. Inside would be a different matter. The goggles powered on, Agent X was able to view the building and lawn in precise, if entirely green, detail. He could see the slight indentation of his path across the lawn, including the dog poop he had apparently stepped in en route. Agent X wiped his foot and whispered into his shoulder mic, "At garage entrance now. Preparing to implement Operation Beddy-Bye."

Back in Steve's backyard, Agent Weisz relayed this to Agent Rajput and Sheila, "He's at the garage entrance now."

Agent X found the side door to the garage unlocked. The pitch black interior and silence indicated it was empty. He slipped inside with more of that no-colour-in-particular cat-like grace.

"Once inside," Rajput explained with confidence, "our Agent will begin the simple process of chloroforming the house's four occupants."

"Four? Including the baby?" asked Sheila with surprise.

Rajput and Weisz stepped aside for a moment to discuss before Rajput agreed, "Probably not the baby."

Agent X studied the garage interior exposed in the verdant glow of the goggles. For the most part, the garage contained exactly the items one would expect; parked car, toolset, unused exercise equipment ordered from late night infomercials, etc. The surprise was the massive tarpaulin draped structure directly blocking his way. Agent X looked at the brightly illuminated door frame leading to the house on the opposite side. He didn't care what the object was, only that it was in his way. "There appears to be some sort of object blocking my path," he whispered into his radio. "Preparing to circumvent."

"Some sort of obstacle in his path. He says, he's 'preparing to circumvent'," related Weisz.

"Circumvent—what exactly does that mean?" asked Sheila.

"He'll climb over it," explained Rajput.

Agent X felt the solid wooden frame through the tarp, then pulled himself on top. In his head, he briefly theorized what it felt like and decided with confidence he knew exactly what it was. Why Parks was building a picnic table he had no idea, but it hardly mattered, he decided.

"So, once Agent X is inside the house," asked Sheila, "how long do you expect the rest of the operation to take?"

Agent X was surprised to discover that the apparent picnic table was incomplete as his hand plunged through an opening. He caught and dragged himself up over an odd, bowl-like mechanism.

"The entire operation will proceed like clockwork as each occupant is rendered unconscious in turn," explained Rajput. He then added with a chuckle, "To put it simply, they won't know what hit them."

Agent X reached forward for something to grasp through the black tarpaulin. He found himself gripping what seemed to be some sort of upwards wooden bar. He attempted to pull himself forward but discovered, much to his surprise, that the bar moved. In a lever-like motion, thought Agent X, what an odd picnic table this–

With a massive "SPROING!" the catapult's arm was released, sending Agent X and his thoughts blasting through the roof of the garage. In a moment of bewildered surprise Agent X found himself high above the Parks and Prefect homes and crowded street below. He had a perfect view of the brightly lit neighbourhood and crowds of people. Someone had ordered Pizza he noted, as he could see the delivery man looking for the customer and the customer waiting down the street, but neither could see each other. It was exactly like having an out-of-body experience, he decided, except that his body had come with him.

Of course, in Steve Prefect's backyard, nobody had yet put two and some imaginary number together to figure out what had happened. To them, the plan was still proceeding exactly as expected. Agent Rajput stood before the aquamarine glow of Steve's swimming pool, completing his answer to Sheila's question. "In fact, I think it's safe to say, Walter Parks is probably being chloroformed right about..." Rajput glanced at his watch for effect, "...now."

At that moment a piercing scream could be heard from above. Its direction and amplitude made it seem like the scream of a falling World War II bomb. Its inflection, however, made it sound far more human. It was, of course, Agent X who had decided to stop trying to figure how he had ended up a hundred feet in the air and instead focus on the Earth rushing up to meet him there.

Before anyone on the ground could make up their minds as to what exactly was coming, Agent X exploded into the swimming pool with an enormous splash, soaking everyone, and ruining several suits in the process. After a stunned pause, agents and officers rushed to help the operative who now floundered in the chlorinated water, stammering, and spitting.

Agent Rajput also snapped into action. Turning to Sheila, he asked, "Um... we can edit this part out, yes?"

CHAPTER 15

"I'm fixing a hole where the rain gets in,
and stops my mind from wandering." - Noah

The morning sun streamed down on Walter as he stood staring at the hole in his garage roof. He considered whether it was at all plausible that the garage had always had an open-air skylight, and he'd simply not noticed it. Of course, the released arm of the catapult below certainly suggested the cause but what, exactly, had been flung through the roof was a mystery. He'd conducted a quick role call of the residence and everyone was accounted for. Still, the cartoonishly man-shaped nature of the hole was unsettling.

"I think you can build your trebuchet now," observed Sancho. Sancho, who had climbed up on the roof to examine the hole from the other side, now looked down at Walter from above.

"Yes," said Walter, "I suppose that's true."

"Breakfast!" called Dawn from the kitchen.

Sancho stood up on the roof and looked around the castle walls. The police and FBI surrounded them on all four sides, while the crowds of onlookers were confined to the street. There was no indication that any sort of missile had been launched among them. In Steve Prefect's swimming pool he noticed what appeared to be a snorkelling mask floating forgotten. Sancho shrugged and climbed down the ladder to the lawn below. He'd been up all night on guard duty and was looking forward to getting some breakfast and going to bed.

* * *

Sancho entered the kitchen to find Walter at the breakfast table watching CNN with the sound off. On screen, CNN Anchor John King was drawing with his finger on 'the big board'. He drew pink x's to indicate the FBI positions and blue o's to represent the Police. Walter, Sancho realized, was taking notes. Jesus jumped up to sniff excitedly at Sancho's crotch.

"Jesus stop that!" shouted Walter, grabbing the dog's collar. "If Jesus starts sniffing your crotch like that don't be afraid to yell at him. It's a bad habit."

"Is okay," said Sancho.

Dawn began serving bacon and eggs onto plates.

Jesus turned and looked at Walter with remorseful eyes. Walter shook his head and scratched the dog behind the ears. "Jesus, you know I can't stay mad at you."

As Sancho sat, Dawn placed plates before him and Walter. She then turned to leave without saying a word.

"You not eating, sweetheart?" asked Walter.

"I'm not hungry."

"Sweetness, you need to eat."

"Yes, is very important," Sancho agreed, munching on a piece of bacon.

"No. Thank you," said Dawn. Clearly unhappy, she turned and left.

Walter considered following her, but there was nothing more to say. Nothing had changed. "She's worried about the baby," he explained.

"Yes," Sancho agreed.

The two men began to eat in earnest. John King had begun drawing hypothetical arrows around the X's and O's of various maneuvers that the Police and FBI might make. Like all news coverage of long term events where nothing much was actually going on, most of the coverage consisted of things that hadn't actually happened and likely never would. In this particular instance, however, his musings had happened. By pure coincidence, his drawing perfectly replicated the third quarter of SuperBowl XVI with the Police as the San Francisco 49ers and the FBI as the Cincinnati Bengals.

"Do you have any kids, Sancho?" asked Walter.

"No."

"Well, someday you will and you'll be able to tell them about this, and they'll say you were crazy."

Sancho grinned. The two men ate for a moment more in silence. CNN switched to an interview with an older Mexican woman. The caption read 'Consuelo Panza'. Sancho's eyes went wide, and he grew instantly agitated. "Turn it up! Turn it up!" he cried.

"What? Why" asked Walter as he reached for the remote.

"Is my madre!"

"Your mother?"

"Si!"

Walter clicked the remote. The woman, Walter realized, did look like an older female version of Sancho. She spoke in Spanish while an English translator repeated her words. "...and pray that he will be safe. He has always been a good boy, and we miss him very much."

Walter thought for a moment that the translator's deep male voice sounded strangely familiar, but let it go. CNN switched back to John King whose onscreen diagrams now coincidently mapped a very small portion of the human genome, where the FBI were adenine and the Police were guanine. John King turned to face the camera, "That was Consuelo Panza from Tijuana, Mexico, whose son, Sancho, is part of the two-man garrison of the besieged Parks family home."

Sancho looked devastated.

"We now return to our live coverage in New Jersey," John King continued, "where our twenty-four-hour 'Parkswatch' continues on this amazing story..." The video switched to a circling aerial shot of the house. Members of the Dream Street crowd held up letters that read "Free Malter Parks." Whoever was holding the "W" had apparently turned to speak with someone behind them.

Walter studied the strain on his friend's face. "Sancho, you should go. Tell them, I mislead you and you didn't mean to do anything illegal. Put the blame on me."

"I want to help you win, sir," said Sancho.

"Your family needs you, Sancho."

Walter looked at him earnestly; he could see the man's resolve weakening. He felt the sudden full weight of responsibility for where he had led Sancho and where he had led his family. "There is no 'win', Sancho, only delaying the inevitable." Sancho was deeply troubled, a man of principle caught between two beliefs, now in opposition. "Look, Sancho, I've taken advantage of you, and–"

Sancho stopped him with a raised hand. "No, Sir Walter," he said, "I am not blind. I am not a foolish boy. I knew what I was doing."

Despite Sancho's protest Walter could not believe it was true. He knew that even when he had told Sancho to go at the beginning, he had secretly hoped he would stay. He could have driven Sancho away, but he'd never truly tried. "Sancho, this is about me and my family, that's it. There is no grand meaning in all of it. It's all nonsense. And now we've managed to drag you and your family in with us. It's a mistake. I'm looking after mine, and you need to look after yours. I'm just a guy out of work and you're just a clerk I met in a store. That's all there is, that's all there ever was."

Sancho stood up from the table with a sudden rush of anger, "And I tell you, you are wrong, sir! You think because I am just clark from Mexico, because my English is imperfect, that I am a fool?"

"Clerk."

"What?"

"You're a clerk. You said "Clark", like your name is Clark."

"I know what I am. But, my point was that I am no fool."

"No, of course not!"

"You see them?" demanded Sancho, pointing to the TV. "You see what they say?"

Walter looked at the TV. The letter holders had become hopelessly rearranged in the press of the crowd. "Wearers Fart kelP? What does that even mean?"

Sancho threw up his arms and stormed from the room.

"Sancho!" Walter called after him as he rose to his feet to follow.

* * *

Walter found Sancho at the top of the front wall. Sancho gazed out to the street and did not look down when Walter called out from below. "Sancho, look I'm sorry. I understand that you wanted to believe in something..."

Sancho shook his head and smiled without taking his gaze from beyond the street. "You see? I am not wrong, it is you who are wrong."

"Sancho..."

"Come look," said Sancho, waving him up. Walter hesitated. "Look!" Sancho insisted.

Walter sighed and climbed the ladder to the wall-walk behind the battlements. Once atop the wall, he looked out at the now familiar scene of the surrounding encampments.

"There he is! It's Parks!" shouted someone in the crowd. Walter looked at the dozens of police cars, barricades, and FBI vehicles. He looked at the muddy mess around the moat where a few discarded helmets and riot shields lay were they'd fallen.

"Yes, I've made a royal mess of things," said Walter.

"No, there!" Sancho pointed past the first ring of police and past the second ring of news media to the motley masses of anxious neighbours and strangers pressed against the wooden police barriers. Somehow he pointed in the massive throng of people to a single woman who held a sign that read 'We believe in you Walter.' A few feet from her Walter noticed a man waving a sign that read 'Parks for President'. Despite the distance and obvious impossibility of the message, Walter saw earnest hope in the man's eyes. Next Walter saw a family of four, all wearing T-shirts with Walter's face printed on them in what appeared to be a knock-off of the famous Che Guevara print. Feet away, a group held a banner that read "Don't give up Walter!" Walter suddenly saw all of the hundreds of faces looking at him with a mix of expectation and awe. They knew what he did not—*what he was doing and why.*

"Walter!... Walter!... Walter!" some of the crowd began to chant at the sight of him.

"Now you see?" asked Sancho, "Now you see?"

Walter saw a small child, held in her mother's arms, looking at him with wonder and found himself whispering, "Now I see."

* * *

One hour later the drawbridge descended for the first time in three days. The crowd gasped in surprise at the sound of the rattling chains which signaled the opening of the door. They gasped again at the site of the lone figure standing there, framed by the castle gate. News cameras turned, and flash bulbs flashed as Sancho crossed the moat with arms raised, "I give up! I give up!" he cried.

As soon as he stood on solid ground, the drawbridge raised swiftly once more. The police grasped the opportunity too late and charged forward only to reach the moat's edge just as the gate sealed more.

Fourteen police officers piled on Sancho, pushing him violently to the ground and hand-cuffing him. A few officers reflexively drew their tasers before realizing that electrocuting the clearly submissive man in front of so much news media might not be properly perceived.

Sheila reported in voiceover while Bob captured the entire scene on camera. "A startling development here on day three as Parks's confederate Sancho leaves Parks Castle apparently of his own free will. A tactic, a deal, or perhaps even a falling out, we don't yet know."

As Sheila spoke, Sancho was dragged roughly to his feet and lead away to one of the police cruisers. Members of the crowd both cheered and jeered him in confused excitement. Some cheered Sancho the man, while others cheered his being arrested. Others jeered Sancho, while still others jeered the police. The crowd was largely confused by what it felt and how to express it. Some resorted to noncommittal noise-making designed to express emotional investment, while refusing to participate in any actual show of support either way that might be misinterpreted.

Sheila stepped into frame, as Sancho was whisked away behind her. "It is still unclear as to how much this suspect was a willing participant in the siege or what was his exact role. One thing is clear, there have been vocal calls to revoke his green card and send him back to Mexico. Lets see how the crowd feels about this dramatic turn of events..."

Sheila turned and extended the microphone to a nearby man wearing a Carl's Jr. baseball cap. "I just think that it's wrong that you have an immigrant here taking good castle-building jobs away from Americans," he said. Behind him, another man began to punch the air and shout "USA! USA!" The rest of the crowd joined in, many unsure why they were chanting but happy to do so none-the-less.

CHAPTER 16

"The only good regulation is a dead regulation." - R. Reagan

The Sheriff met Agents Rajput and Weisz bearing news and a pair of submarine sandwiches. He handed the subs to the agents and reported, "Sancho's not saying much, other than that 'Sir' Walter Parks is a 'hero'." The Sheriff made air quotes with his fingers as he said the words "sir" and "hero".

"We'll find out what he knows," Agent Rajput smirked with confidence.

"Good luck with that but, just so you know, we in the Plansville PD know what we're doing when it comes to questioning suspects."

"Is it kosher?" asked Agent Weisz.

"Oh sure, mostly it just involves good cop, bad cop, turning up the thermostat, and withholding drinking water for a couple of hours at a time."

"No, the sandwich."

"Oh yeah, yeah, it's fine."

"Mmm-hmm," smirked Rajput. "Well, let's just say, with us our little Mexican friend won't be 'bored for lack of water'."

The Sheriff nodded knowingly, then realized he had no idea what was Rajput was referring to. "So you don't withhold water?" he asked.

"What? No, we don't withhold water," Rajput said with a wink.

"You should try that."

"Right."

"I think there's ham in here..." said Weisz prying apart the bread. "You said this was kosher?"

"Oh *that* kind of kosher," said the Sheriff, "I thought you just meant, is it good?"

"Regardless," said Rajput, "in this particular case we have an even more effective threat."

"Oh really?" said the Sheriff taking a bite of his sandwich. "Yes, definitely ham. Honey roasted actually. You should try it. You might like it."

Weisz rolled his eyes and threw his sandwich in the trash.

"That is such a waste!" said the Sheriff, aghast.

"If he doesn't talk, we'll threaten..." said Rajput, revealing his fifth ace with a smile, "...to deport his family."

"I thought his family was in Mexico."

Agents Rajput and Weisz exchanged knowing glances before Agent Rajput leaned forward and whispered into the Sheriff's ear. "Not anymore."

"No kidding!" said the Sheriff, spitting food in surprise.

"No kidding," said the annoyed agent, wiping his cheek in disgust.

"Oy vey!" said Agent Weisz. Agent Rajput noticed the shock in his colleague's voice and followed his gaze. The Sheriff took the opportunity to retrieve Weisz's discarded sandwich without anyone noticing. As he did, he heard the low rumble of heavy motorized vehicles. He turned to see a long caravan of green humvees and troop trucks. The US Army had arrived. The crowd, police and agents all stared in a consensus of stunned silence. The Sheriff wiped off Weisz's sandwich and took a bite. "Well boys, I'd say it looks like you just lost yur dicks too," he scoffed with satisfaction.

At the end of the parade rolled two massive mountains of metal. It was a pair of M1 Abrams tanks that cracked the concrete under their weight while being chased by a pack of yipping neighbourhood dogs. An overly ambitious pekinese performed a compelling live reenactment of the 1989 scene from Tiananmen Square. At the last moment, it was snatched from harm's way by its owner, narrowly averting a follow-up performance as an Ikea throw-rug.

The caravan was led by a single jeep and, standing tall in the jeep, chewing on a genuine Conestoga stogie, was General Marshal Heimlich. The General raised his hand and the long train of vehicles rolled to a precise stop. General Heimlich jumped down in front of the three men with all the confidence of an athletic man wearing comfortable shoes. He pulled out his cigar with relish and demanded to know, "You the girls in charge of this little gang-bang?"

"Yes, sir!" shouted Rajput, overwhelmed by the shear testosterone the General radiated.

The General smirked, spat the tobacco he'd been chewing at the same time, and wiped his chin. "Not anymore," he said.

* * *

Steve watched through his front windows as General Heimlich barked orders at his men who, in turn, instantly leapt into action surrounding Parks's house. Steve was almost giddy with excitement at the scene. Walter's in serious dog poop now, he thought. In his mind's eye, it was only a matter of time before his neighbour's house was a smoking crater. He was so electrified, that it wasn't until the third ring that he heard his own phone. He picked up the receiver, still transfixed by the scene outside. "Hello?" he said absently.

"Steve? Tom Paulson."

"Mr. Paulson, sir!" said Steve, wrenched instantly back to reality. The man at the other end of the phone was Thomas Paulson, head of Goldsmith Price Securities and, ultimately, Steve's boss. He was the kind of man who made more in his annual bonus than most people make in their lifetimes, even in an "off year". Tom Paulson kept his money in an off-shore account in a small island country known only as A664-47B-001-1998. A664, as it was called for short, was the only privately held country in the world. The name was originally selected as a simple business number but had the added benefit of foiling any attempts by journalists to report on its existence. News reporters who attempted to discuss island A664-47B-001-1998 discovered that, by the time they had successfully stated the country's entire name, their audience had turned the channel to watch inebriated wealthy women from Orange County argue about shoes.

"I need you to stop making such a damn baboon of yourself," said Mr. Paulson. Mr. Paulson was at that moment standing in his office in Manhattan, surrounded on three sides by panoramic views of New York City. On some days he would strip naked and stand before the one-way glass, declaring himself "God of New York", but not today. Today, he had to meet with the Secretary of the Treasury who preferred his meetings clothed. First, however, Paulson had to speak with the imbecilic Steve Prefect. He spoke with Steve via the speakerphone on his desk, while at the same time he carefully gauged his swing. One side of his office housed the only indoor miniature golf course on Wall Street. Of course, other executives had putting strips, or even small greens in their offices, but only Paulson's course included nine holes, sand traps and the object of his current concentration, a miniature working windmill. This was the hardest hole. It included a steep slope up to the base of the windmill, where a small tunnel entrance was repeatedly blocked by the swift rotation of the blades. The windmill itself was of Spanish design, made with actual parts flown in from Europe. It was a hard shot that most of his guests failed, but Paulson never did, even when holding a critical conversation. This, he'd say to himself, is why I make the big bucks. *This* is why I am the God of New York.

"I'm sorry sir... have I been making a baboon of myself?"

"And of this firm."

"I'm sorry, sir, I had no idea," said Steve, his voice cracking. Steve was now pacing nervously in his living room, completely oblivious to the sandbag barriers being assembled outside by US Army troops. A pair of soldiers began digging a trench across Steve's front lawn.

Paulson sighed, delaying his putt. "Steve, when you go in front of the cameras ranting about this Parks fool you represent us as well."

"But sir, I know why–"

"You don't know diddley-squat," snarled Paulson. "Now, listen up. It seems we, Goldsmith Price Securities, have become the owners of Parks's mortgage. We obtained it from the Wang Hui Tau Bank of Hong Kong in a securities swap deal just before this all blew up. Of course, it came in with about ten thousand other mortgages, so we didn't know it ourselves until today."

There was a momentary pause as this sunk in.

"So... we own Walter Parks's house?"

"Yes. This means we now we have a PR nightmare on our hands. We can't get rid of it as no one else wants it, and it's only a matter of time before some reporter, like a boll weevil with a nose-job, sniffs it out."

"But... but... but, I don't see how..." stammered Steve.

"He's become too popular you idiot! The last thing we can afford to do is look like some big corporate behemoth that doesn't care about the little guy. Not when we're lobbying to get more regulation wriggle-room through in Washington."

Paulson shook his head and, without a moment's hesitation, gently swung the putter, sending the golf ball sailing between the blades and through the tunnel. The ball rolled to a rest inches from the hole.

"I had no idea, sir," said Steve who at this point was clutching nervously at his own hair. Until this moment, he'd imagined his whole career as a meteoric rise. Now, however, he realized meteors traveled down, not up. What travels up? He fretted, desperately searching for a more directionally favourable metaphor for his life.

"Right, well, if you want to keep working for this firm, you need to make nice with Walter Parks. Tell that nice piece-of-ass Channel 8 news lady you want another interview. Tell her how you sympathize with the plight of hardworking Americans like Walter Parks and sound like you mean it!"

Tom Paulson sunk the easy putt and lined up his sights on the next hole, the rhino. The rhino featured an actual white rhino from Africa, poached, stuffed, and neatly posed to offer a challenging final hole right between its legs.

"Yes, sir," grovelled Steve. "But don't we want Walter Parks to go?"

"Of course," said Paulson. "Eventually. Just remember, the news media have all the attention of a kangaroo with RLS, as they say."

"Yes, sir," said Steve. "You can count on me."

"Good," said Paulson.

Steve, in a daze, gently hung up the phone. Outside, an Abrams tank rolled past his window, flattening his bird feeder.

CHAPTER 17

"Read my blog and despair." - O. Mandias

Dawn cradled Hope in her arms, gently swaying her. To anyone else, Hope would have appeared to be a healthy, normal sleeping baby, but Dawn had the mother's eye. She could tell that Hope was faltering. Her cheeks weren't quite as pink and she didn't stir in quite the same way. Dawn had done everything the doctor had ordered and, of course, she had prayed. She knew, however, that faith alone was not enough. After all, the Lord helps those who help themselves. To Dawn, that meant do everything you can do and then have faith.

"I'm really worried about her, Walter."

Walter was sitting beside her on couch, but his eyes were locked on the TV in the corner. CNN panned past the crowds of onlookers on the street outside. Walter could have seen them in person from the upstairs window, but not up close like this, in HD. Sancho's voice echoed in his head, "You the king, Walter, you the king!"

"She looks fine," Walter assured her. "You worry too much."

"You didn't even look at her!"

On TV a pair of crowd members held up a banner that read, "We believe in you Walter!" The camera panned to another supporter holding a cardboard sign, "Fight for US!"

"The Lord of all you survey," Sancho whispered in Walter's mind. Imaginary Sancho then said something about wanting a burrito for lunch, but Walter ignored that. They believe in me. Walter wallowed in the warmth of those words. It was a Jacuzzi of a thought — the kind that makes you feel good and turns your muscles to rubber. Nobody had ever *believed* in Walter before. He'd heard "I believe you're wrong" and "I believe you're a complete idiot", but never in a good way. Believe, he thought, is a funny word. Then, he thought, I believe in me.

"I am the King," said Walter, and he rose to his feet in an epiphanic daze.

"What?"

Walter turned to leave.

"Walter, where are you going?"

"To the bedroom," he said and then, as if no further explanation were required, he did.

* * *

Walter opened the closet door and pushed aside his dress pants to reveal the large blue travel trunk hidden behind. He dragged the chest out into the open, flipped the brass latch and opened the lid. Inside was a poster for the original Medieval Times—"It's a great knight out!" Walter lifted the carefully preserved poster and placed it aside. Beneath was a historically accurate knight's costume. The ensemble included real chainmail, steel chest plate, helmet, shield and, of course, sword. Walter felt like a knight returning to his lair. Did knights have lairs? Batman did, and he was sort of a knight. Walter reached in and lifted the sword. He imagined he was not so much lifting it as receiving it from the Lady of the Lake, or in the case, the Lady of the Closet. In a moment of inspiration, he proclaimed "I am the king!" and thrust the sword aloft. The sword tip stabbed into the ceiling plaster, raining dust and paint down onto Walter's head. "Pfft!" he said, as he plucked paint powder from his tongue.

"Are you all right?" called Dawn from the living room.

"I'm fine," answered Walter.

* * *

General Heimlich leaned back in his chair with his feet on his desk and the confidence of a king. He felt like Napoleon, only taller and less French. Around him, enlisted men scurried to set up the rest of his operations tent. The chair and desk were the first things. Everything else, *everyone else*, was scenery.

Before him stood local Sheriff what's-his-name, and FBI Agents Jewish-guy and Indian-fella. Times they were a-changin', but the idiocy remained the same. One of the General's favourite things about the military was you didn't need to remember people's names. It was either "Sir", "Colonel", or "Hey you—yes, you, dickwad." The General stuck a burning match in the bowl of his corncob pipe and sucked. The pipe had once been owned by General Douglas MacArthur. "All right, first things first, we get Parks on the phone and let him know who he's dealing with. Sound good ladies?"

The Sheriff raised a tentative finger, "General Heimlich, I...um..."

"Yes, what is it?"

The Sheriff gathered himself together like a trilobite desperately trying to imagine what a spine would be like, had they been evolved yet. "Well, General, it's just that I'm a decorated police officer with twenty-years on the force and..."

"And? And what?"

"Well, General... I, we, don't appreciate being addressed in a... well, a feminine manner."

"A feminine manner?" said the General incredulously. "A feminine manner? Well, Jesus Christ, man, if the dress fits!"

"General..." said Agent Rajput in a meek effort to show unity.

The General cast his mind back to the 'sensitivity training courses' he'd been required to take more than once. In the military they trained you in a hundred ways to kill a man, but heaven forbid you slap him on the ass first. It was all harmless fun, camaraderie if you will, but it could send even a four-star general in for a week of Powerpoints and 'real life' examples. "Ah, don't get yur panties in a knot," said the General dismissively. "Speakin' of which..." the General adjusted his own undergarments and smiled satisfactorily at the result. "Much better."

As if on queue, a Private entered the tent holding out a cellphone. "General, we have Parks on the line."

"Excellent," said the General as he took the phone. "Now let's see what this pansy-boy does when big daddy tells him to bend over and take it." The General put the phone to his ear with a confident smile. A moment later his smile flattened, "Uh-huh? Everything? Damn, I thought it was on mute."

"There is no mute button, sir," said the Private.

"Thank you, Private. Now if you can just go back in time and stick that up your ass, that would be great." General Heimlich turned his attention back to the phone call. "Now, where were we? Oh yes. So Parks, you're dealing with the US Army now. My name is General Heimlich." The Sheriff and two FBI agents watched as Heimlich listened. The General smiled, "Oh yes? Well, I'm flattered." The General covered the receiver and told them, "He says he's a big fan of my maneuvers. I had no idea civilians followed such things."

The four waiting men exchanged blank expressions.

* * *

Walter stood in front of the bathroom mirror, now dressed entirely in the knight's armour. He cradled the phone against his ear as he attached the scabbard to his belt. Cool, he thought even as he listened to General Heimlich. He could see Jesus watching him in the mirror from behind. Jesus wagged his tail. Even Jesus thinks I look cool, he thought. "I understand General, but I'm exercising my right to defend my home."

Jesus sniffed at the scabbard tip before deciding it was definitely "some kind of a stick" and chomped on it.

"Jesus, stop it! Stop it!" Walter scolded the dog, waggling his finger a him.

Jesus looked at Walter plaintively and licked his gauntleted hand.

"That's okay, boy. Good boy," said Walter reassuringly, before realizing the General had been talking. "I'm sorry, General, what was that?"

* * *

The General scowled with annoyance. He was not used to being ignored. That was the problem with telephones, they lacked the personal touch that only face-to-face intimidation could bring. The General glanced at his small audience in the tent. He was determined not to show any weakness. "Now, you listen here Parks, either you come out in the next hour, or we're coming in."

The General paused to allow Walter a moment to surrender. Instead, he heard only strange noises and strange utterances about Jesus before Walter asked him to repeat himself. "I said we're coming in." The four men watching tried to make sense of the one side of the conversation they could hear. "No, in the next hour... Yes, sixty minutes, that's right... From when we hang up, fine." The General hung up the phone, shook his head, and looked grimly at the Private, the policeman and the two agents. "The man is clearly insane," he said as he paused to suck on his pipe and blow smoke in their faces. "Not only is he not coming out, but he keeps complaining that Jesus is humping his leg."

CHAPTER 18

"Anyone got a light?" - Max Pruss

One hour later, Walter sat once more on the sofa beside Dawn. Now, however, Walter was in full armour, complete with sword and shield. The only item he did not wear was his helmet, which was hot and heavy. Instead, it sat upside down on the coffee table before him, full of Pringles potato chips.

Walter munched on a Pringle. He then glanced at his watch. There was still twenty minutes to go. CNN had gone to a commercial for "FreeCreditReport.com". Walter wondered how a business could afford expensive commercials to tell people about a free service. He assumed there was a catch. Walter wondered where the line was between marketing and swindling.

Walter glanced at his watch again, nineteen minutes to go.

* * *

General Heimlich stood alone, facing the castle walls. He'd told the men to stand back. He needed a moment to get a sense of the enemy. He stood now at the edge of the moat where so many good men had fallen and become very, very damp. He hadn't seen it himself, but the footprints in the mud and occasional lost piece of police-issue footwear told of the carnage—*the horror.* Opposite him stood the closed drawbridge, upright—as if Walter Parks himself were lifting a giant wooden finger to America. On this side of the moat was Walter's mailbox. It was stuffed to the point of overflow with coupon booklets and menus from local Thai restaurants. Walter had been unable to collect his mail for days. "What kind of freedom is that?" the General wondered. He picked up and pocketed a Victoria's Secret catalog. That would come in handy later.

"General?"

General Heimlich recognized the Private's voice. He pulled out a small steel tin and extracted a pinch of snuff, enough for each nostril. "Yes?"

The Private moved close enough to speak discretely to the General and even then, he whispered. With the media leveling dozens of parabolic microphones at them, one could never be too cautious. Loose-lips sink ships and the Private wouldn't be the one caught on camera saying something unfortunate. "Sir, only fifteen minutes left, should we prepare for attack?"

"No, no, no, that's hours away," said the General as he snorted the finely powdered tobacco.

"But you told Parks he had sixty minutes."

The General gave a derisive snort. "It's called *the element of surprise*, Private."

"Um, okay..." The Private considered this for moment. He turned it around and around in his head like a Chinese puzzle, unable to make sense of it from any angle. "But, sir, wouldn't it be more of a surprise if we went in early, rather than late?"

The General glared at the junior officer who immediately wanted to suck his words back up into his mouth. "How many stars have you got on your lapel, Private?"

"None, sir."

"And how many do I have?"

"Four, sir."

The General double-checked, then nodded and said, "Exactly."

"Yes, sir."

The General considered pinning the Private to the ground like an alpha-male dog showing his superiority. He'd done it before, but then he considered the cameras and large crowd of civilians and decided against it. Besides, the Private seemed suitably cowed.

At that moment, a cheer went up from the crowd. General Heimlich turned to see that Walter Parks had appeared at the top of the wall. The General stared at him incredulously.

"Is he wearing a suit of armour?"

"Plate armour, sir," said the Private. "With some chainmail beneath. Probably fourteenth century, Greenwich design."

"Including a codpiece."

"Yes, sir."

"Uh-huh..." said the General. "He looks good."

"Parks, sir?"

General Heimlich nodded, "The suit, it fits him very well. Very... manly. I like it."

"Yes, sir."

"You'd look good in it too, Private."

"Thank you, sir."

Behind the police-lines the crowd began to chant, "Walter! Walter! Walter!..."

Walter and the General exchanged long stares. For a moment it was just the two of them, worthy adversaries sizing each other up before the battle. Walter broke the spell when he took off his helmet to brush Pringle chip crumbs from his hair.

The tumult of the crowd grew louder, and Walter broke gazes with the General to acknowledge it. He raised his sword in the air where it caught the sunlight and flashed. The crowd roared their approval, and newspapers around the world got their cover shots.

* * *

Three hours later Walter and General Heimlich still stood in their respective places. The General's plan was to psychologically wear Walter down. Walter's plan was to balance his sword pommel on the palm of his hand. The news media had already been worn down. After intense speculation of an impending battle, they had switched to yet another recap of the situation, followed by a commercial break, another recap, and finally they had resorted to other news, including the weather.

Apparently there was flooding in Texas and fourteen families had lost their homes.

Dawn climbed the ladder to the top of the wall beside Walter. She did so while carrying a sandwich and a glass of milk. "I brought you lunch, Walter."

"Oh thank you, sweetheart," said Walter, eagerly taking the food. "I'm starving."

"Walter, I'm really worried about–"

"Honey, please, not in front of the mob."

Dawn started to protest, but saw that Walter had already forgotten she was there. He was studying the people outside the walls while trying to fit the sandwich under his helmet, and succeeding only in smearing mayonnaise everywhere. Shaking her head, Dawn turned and left. Walter finally removed his helmet altogether and began to eat. It was tomato and sardines on rye—his favourite.

The General watched this scene play out from the ground below. He could not hear what was said, but sensed the moment. He lifted his hand to beckon the Private, who immediately rushed over. "It's time," he said.

The Private nodded and jogged over to a sergeant where he relayed the order. "Fall in!" screamed the Sergeant.

The soldiers snapped to position and climbed into their humvees and tanks. The news media interrupted their sports casts, and millions of eyes returned to Dream Street once more. "Forward at ready!" screeched the Sergeant. He then said something else, but it was drowned out by the roar of engines starting and the murmurs of the excited crowd.

"It looks like this is it!" said Sheila, eagerly picking up her mic.

The Siege of Walter Parks

Walter disappeared from sight behind the wall.

* * *

In the course of the seemingly endless face-off between General Heimlich and Walter, various news outlets had decided to send their helicopters off for refuelling. This meant that, for the first time since the siege had begun, there were no helicopters aloft to view the inside of the castle walls. If there had been, they would have seen Walter climb down the ladder and run, half tripping over his long sword, across the lawn, and around to the side of the house. There the American Dream billboard, once an eyesore on the front lawn of Walter's home, now leaned against the wall, sawed off at the posts. Walter crouched under the lean-to thus created, where a row of gasoline barrels stood concealed. He knew exactly how medieval castle garrisons had defended themselves from attack. Most of the methods were either impractical or simply too dangerous. Pouring hot oil from the walls could really hurt someone, while flinging dead animals into the crowd was downright disgusting. Walter wanted to repel his besiegers, not harm them. He turned on a valve pump connected to the first barrel and watched as the attached hose jumped with turgid life.

Satisfied he ran tripping back to the front wall.

* * *

The soldiers finished their rapid assembly of battering rams on the front of their humvees. It was the General's strategy to fight medieval fire with fire, as it were. He'd wanted to launch sheep over the castle walls, but apparently the livestock-lovers at the SPCA considered that "animal cruelty", especially if the sheep were still alive. The General had tried to argue that what the animals would experience would, for the most part, be a thrilling ride akin to hang-gliding or bungee-jumping. He pointed out that only the last bit would be unpleasant. Still, his arguments had fallen on deaf ears. His other plan had been to mine tunnels beneath the castle walls. He discovered, however, that the municipal permits required to tunnel under a neighbour's defences in New Jersey took weeks for approval and would have to be built to code. Oddly enough, the activities of sappers were, in fact, explicitly covered by state by-laws. So in the end he was left with the battering rams. He admired the long row of humvees with the eight-foot rams thrust forward and slightly upward. Suddenly, he felt more excited than he'd ever felt before.

"Now, sir?" asked the Private.

"Not yet," said the General. "I want to see the look on his face."

It had been several minutes since Walter had disappeared from the parapets.

"How do we know he's coming back, sir?"

"Oh, we know... we know," said General Heimlich with confidence. As if on queue, Walter's head poked up from between the sawtooth merlons that topped the castle wall. "You see! Walter Parks, and I think alike."

"I thought you said he was crazy, sir."

"Don't be ridiculous," scowled the General. "I can tell he's a warrior like me. A man's man. Homo Erectus. Mano a Mano."

"You do know that 'mano a mano' means hand to hand sir, not man to man."

"It means what I say it means."

"Of course, sir."

The General tried to meet Walter's gaze. He wanted to see the look on the man's face as the army penetrated his defences and bent him over into submission. Walter, however, would not cooperate. He was more interested in adjusting his chainmail skirt which had ridden up in ways that were beyond uncomfortable and wondering if Sir Lancelot ever had to pull steel links out from between his buttocks. Annoyed, General Heimlich turned to face his own forces and raised his hand. "Ready, one, two, three... attack!" For a moment, there was stunned confusion. General Heimlich never counted to three and then said "attack", it was too "expected". During war games, he would count to any number other than three then yell "attack". The idea was to keep his men on their toes. They needed to be ready to attack at any moment. To this end, he once yelled attack in the middle of a speech on latrine safety with no count at all. The result was a confused mess and six weeks of hard basic-training review for the men. Another time he counted to one-thousand three-hundred and seventy-five. Half of the men were nodding off when the moment came, leading to another six weeks of drills. The men had grown to anticipate that the order to attack could come at any possible moment, except, after a count of three. After a moment's surprised pause however, they snapped to action and collectively prayed that the General would not consider the delay long enough to be worth punishing.

The General dropped his arm to point at the castle walls, and thus avoid any confusion as to where the attack was to be directed. The line of armoured humvees rolled forward. The initial thought was to charge the walls quickly and drive the rams through, but there was the intermediary problem of the moat. The fear was that if the humvees moved too quickly, the rams would become lodged in the far lip of the moat and that the humvees would then, owing to their speed and trajectory, flip forward and "turtle" against the castle wall. Computer models provided by Pentagon contractors had confirmed this possible outcome. The advice had been to move slowly and negotiate the opposite bank, before ramming the castle walls. "The walls are made of cinder blocks," the engineer had said, "Seriously, just give me a sledgehammer and I'll do it myself." The computer models had cost over six million dollars to provide. Had all of the humvees been totalled, the cost would have been half a million dollars. Avoiding public humiliation, however, was priceless. The khaki-coloured ring contracted as the humvees approached the moat's edge. Of course, the fact that four Abrams tanks were also included in the assault made the outcome, in the eyes of most, a "forgone conclusion".

From atop the castle walls, Walter squinted. He could just make out the rainbow sheen of gasoline now flooding across the moat's surface. Despite his planning, he had been nervous. Would this stop the attack? Would it even slow them down? He pulled out a book of matches and struck one. He dropped the tiny flame. As it fell, the air motion extinguished it.

"Drat!" said Walter. The humvees were not yet at the water's edge. Walter quickly struck another match and dropped it.

Once more the match went out midway between the wall-top and water's surface.

"Double drat!" said Walter. The humvees' front tires rolled into the water. The rams dipped into the surface like the long noses of two-dozen armour-plated anteaters. Walter panicked and tried to strike another match. This one failed to light altogether. When he tried again, he destroyed it between his armoured fingers. In frustration, he pulled off his gauntlets and dropped them at his feet. He tried another match. It lit, but then slipped between his sweaty fingers and made contact with the remaining matches. The entire book flared into flames. Surprised and in pain, Walter dropped the tiny fireball. He watched as, in apparent slow motion, the burning booklet fell towards the water. The General watched as well, trying to understand exactly what Walter was doing playing with matches at a time like this. That's just plain reckless, he thought. At that moment, the wind shifted and the General caught the clear vaporous smell of gasoline. War and the smell of gasoline, he thought for a moment, that takes me back. Good times. Then, he had another thought —oh... no.

When the burning book of matches was several inches above the moat's surface the fumes caught fire. A flower of yellow flame bloomed outwards and raced swiftly across the water. The soldiers stared through their bulletproof windshields in surprise.

"Retreat! Retreat!" the General screamed. Instantly the vehicles where in full-on panicked reverse. The crowd gasped as they saw that several of the metal armoured vehicles were, inexplicably, on fire. Humvees spun their tires before flying backwards up the banks of the moat. Several of the reversing armoured vehicles plowed into one another. One humvee stalled in the mud, and the crew was forced to abandon it as a burning Abrams tanks rolled backwards over top, pancaking the smaller vehicle.

The entire attack force rolled to a stop, well back from the burning ring of fire that the moat had become. Soldiers rushed forward with extinguishers and began spraying white foam on flaming metal hoods and grills.

General Heimlich, who had once held a greco-roman wrestling match with his men beneath the burning oil wells of Kuwait wearing nothing but a patina of petroleum, was unfazed by the scene. He gazed ruefully at Walter who still stood atop the castle wall, nursing his burnt fingertips. "Very good, Mr. Parks. You've won this battle, but not the war." The General snapped his fingers and beckoned to the nearby private, "Bring me my hookah, I need to think." The Private, who had been helping extract a stunned soldier from the door of a humvee welded shut by fire, dropped the man to attend to the General's order.

An hour later, TV reporter Sheila Blitz stood with microphone in hand before the cleanup of the failed attack. After much digging and pressing the various soldiers for information, she finally had her answer. "We've since learned the reason for army's fast retreat. It seems that the military vehicles have all recently been repainted with paint imported from China. Paint which, while considerably cheaper, it turns out, is also extremely flammable. This is Sheila Blitz, Channel 8 news, reporting."

CHAPTER 19

"She's with my best friend, why?" - A. Pendragon

A sea of flickering flames dotted Dream Street in the night. The growing tide of supporters were holding a candlelight-vigil for the Parks family and singing *We shall overcome.* Like waves, they would loudly sing the chorus, fall away to quietly mumble the stanza in-between (to which no one knew the words), then rise again in a rousing rendition of the refrain.

Sheila Blitz, exhausted from days of near continuous coverage was now running on a mix of Starbucks double-shot espressos and Krispy-Kreme doughnuts. She stood like a zombie in mascara, microphone in hand, addressing the camera once more. Since the siege had begun, she had become a fixture on American TV screens. This was her big break, but right now it felt more like an exercise in sleep-deprivation where the subjects were repeatedly forced to apply fresh eyeliner, sound chipper and act not-at-all deranged for the cameras. In Vegas, some bookies had begun to take bets as to whether Sheila would collapse on camera before the end of the siege. The current odds were four to three against, but shifting.

"And there they are," said Sheila, pointing to the flickering vigil behind her, "like candles in the wind, these ... candles... in the wind. Sheila Blitz, Channel 8, reporting."

Sheila smiled her practiced smile and waited.

"Sheila?" said Bob, waving at her. He was signalling to her that they were no longer live, and she could relax.

"What?"

"We're out."

"Oh right," said Sheila. She realized that she may have actually slept through the last part of her own story. Could one actually report while unconscious? Fox News reporters seemed to do it all the time. She smirked at her own joke. "That didn't sound completely delirious did it?"

"No, no, no, not completely."

"Good." She had been forced to relax her standards for on-camera excellence after the first forty-eight hours. She was damned if she would let those bookies in Vegas win. She was even more damned if she'd let Bob, who had bet against her, win. "Okay, let's get some interviews after the break. Who've we got lined up?"

Sheila turned to see Alfie, one of the Channel 8 crew who had come down to help, standing with a prospective subject. The man wore a long beard, robes and a sandwich board that read in large bold letters,

"There is no US and them."

Sheila rolled her tired eyes. "Okay, can we get someone to interview who's not crazy?"

Sheila went on to find an angry housewife who had also lost her home to the bank. Had she interviewed the "crazy man" with the sandwich board sign she would have found him to be very lucid, intelligent, and the only person in the crowd who completely understood how to resolve the situation and what it all meant. He would have told her his name was Frank. That, however, would have been a lie. His real name was Samuel J. Timmins, or perhaps it was Praxton. The truth was confusing. He could also have told her that he was a virgo, which was almost certainly true, but entirely irrelevant.

* * *

A dozen knights stood in battle ready poses. They clutched swords, pikes, battle axes, and swung morning stars with the spiked balls suspended in midair. A giant knight reached down and picked up one of them, moving him forward so that his outthrust sword stabbed another, knocking the victim over, dead. The giant knight, named Walter, smiled with satisfaction and looked about the dresser-top battlefield for his next subject. "Arthur?" he wondered aloud, "Where's Arthur?"

Walter carefully surveyed the battlefield, but could not see the lilliputian king. Jesus watched Walter from the door of the bedroom. Walter was so intent on finding the missing toy that he did not notice Jesus. Had he done so, he might also have noticed the tiny booted feet protruding from the dog's mouth.

Walter crouched on the floor and peered under the dresser.

"Goddamn it! Where is King Arthur?"

Jesus watched Walter curiously for a moment. He never understood most of what humans did. They made odd and unpredictable noises. They walked around on their hind legs. They had no appreciation for squirrels. Still, Jesus did not judge them, he merely wished they'd stop telling him what to do. Jesus mouthed the curious metal stick he'd found, turned and went out into the hall. "Where the heck could he be?" asked Walter behind him.

Jesus trundled down the hallway enjoying the taste of metal and his own slobber. The stick had a sharp little branch on it. Jesus adjusted it with his tongue, so the tiny sword stuck out from between his lips. Sensing Dawn's presence, he turned and padded into Hope's bedroom.

Hope lay in her crib while Dawn knelt beside her, head bowed in prayer. Dawn's fingers reached between the wooden slats to hold Hope's tiny hand. Jesus watched this all for a moment from the doorway. He watched and chewed slowly on King Arthur's head. He knew Dawn was distressed and had been for days. This in turn had made Jesus distressed. He had tried to cheer her up. It did not work. He tried to cheer himself up by chewing on Walter's toy. That did not seem to help much either. Still, chewing on something was as close to a panacea for sadness as the world had ever found. Perhaps it was simply not being applied in the right place. Jesus cautiously approached Dawn and gently nuzzled her leg. Dawn reached down and petted him. She did so absentmindedly, without looking down and without feeling. Jesus nosed open her palm and placed King Arthur inside. Dawn looked down in surprise at the saliva-coated toy. For a moment she did not recognize it. She then dropped it numbly to the floor and stared again at her own wet palm.

Jesus looked at her in surprise. It was a chew object. The precoating of saliva should have made that clear and made it especially tasty. She must have dropped it by mistake. Jesus picked up the knight and placed it once more in her palm.

"No, Jesus, no," she said. Jesus knew those sounds. Amid the usual nonsense humans babbled were a few words whose meaning was clear and the clearest of all was "no". Jesus heard "no" a lot.

Jesus whimpered and dropped the king at her feet. For a moment, he looked at the odd little stick. It did look like a little human with one hand holding a sword, and the other a crown. Jesus decided to leave it for her there, in case she came to her senses and recognized the value of a good chew. He then turned and left.

Walter was turning over the sofa cushions. So far he'd found a seventeen cents and a pair of nameless serfs, but not King Arthur. He looked about the carpeted landscape for the tiny toy, but saw instead Dawn's feet standing in the doorway. "Have you seen King Arthur anywhere? I think Jesus took him," Walter asked. He dropped once more to his hands and knees and began scanning under the furniture. "I swear that dog leaps up and snatches them right off the dresser. I mean how else could he keep getting them?"

"Walter, it's time to give up."

Walter squinted to see through the shadows and dust bunnies. "Of course, how he does it without knocking the whole thing over, is a miracle to me."

"I said, it's time to give up."

"What? No, I'll find it. Maybe chewed to pieces, but I will find it." Walter gave up on the sofa and cast about for other potential hiding places.

"Walter, it's time to open the drawbridge and give up."

Walter looked at her in surprise. "What? The drawbridge? Why?"

"Have you looked at your daughter lately?"

Walter shook his head and waved her away. "She's fine. The doctor said there might be–"

Dawn stepped in front of him, not prepared to be dismissed so easily. "She's not fine Walter. She's getting worse. We need to give up so she can go to the hospital."

Walter considered this for a moment. He couldn't give up now, not when so many people were counting on him. Jesus entered the room. He once more had King Arthur in his mouth and was chewing on it gently. Dawn had forgotten it in the other room, and Jesus wanted to offer it to her again. Of course, if she really didn't want it...

"She's probably just tired," said Walter.

"She sleeps all the time."

Walter shook his head again. He was getting annoyed now. "You're not a doctor, Dawn, how do you know?" He felt Jesus nuzzling his hand, trying to put something in it. Walter pushed the dog away.

"I can tell. A mother can tell," said Dawn. She looked at her husband who appeared unmoved. She'd never seen him so resolute. "Walter, the whole reason we did this was for Hope. We did it to keep her in her home, so she could get better. We always knew this wouldn't last long. Frankly, it's lasted longer than we could ever have... hoped for."

"No!" Walter spun about with visible anger, "No, no, no. You're just giving up because you want to."

"Walter..."

"You don't think I can win this. Well, the people outside there do! They believe in me." Walter pointed to the wall, but did so vigorously to indicate that he was really pointing at the people beyond the wall. He then waved his arm about in a gesture intended to include all of America, with the exception of perhaps Alaska, which was too far north.

Dawn shook her head, exasperated. Then, she felt something she'd never felt toward her husband before. She felt anger. "They don't even know you! You're just this... idea they believe in."

"You mean they have faith in me? Is that it? Maybe you can't stand that I've become something more than 'old Walter', the nobody. To you I'm just a guy who can't keep his job, but to them, I'm Sir Walter. What I'm doing here means something. I'm the man standing up to those faceless corporations. I'm charging on my steed, and I'm going to bring those sons-of-bitches crashing down! I–"

Dawn stared at him in shock. This wasn't the Walter she knew. He didn't even look like Walter anymore as the anger had flushed his face, turning it beet-red. A small vein then began to throb on Walter's temple.

"I'm leaving and I'm taking Hope with me."

The air in the room turned to ice.

"Fine."

"Fine?"

Walter turned away from her, "Yes, fine, go." He would not lose this fight. He *could not* lose this fight. He was the king, after all.

Dawn wiped tears from her eyes. After staring at Walter's back for a moment in disbelief, she turned and fled the room.

She left in silence and, for a moment, Walter was not sure if she were there or not. He turned to look and stepped on something. Lifting up his foot he saw the tiny figure of King Arthur, now mangled beyond recognition.

CHAPTER 20

"Where the heck did all these dang chickens come from?"
- G.W. Bush

"Is that better?" Sheila faced the camera once more. She had been busily trying to glue down a tuft of stray hair that had decided now, of all times, to misbehave. Evidently, even six applications of hair spray had begun to fail and now she was reduced to wetting her palm and patting it down without the aid of a mirror. The wisp of hair popped up again. "Still sticking up on the left," said Bob with a sigh.

Sheila frantically licked her palm and petted her own head once more, to no effect. "How about now?"

"Um..."

Sheila petted it more vigorously, which only succeeded in making matters worse. "How about now?"

"Much better."

"Really? It feels like it's worse," Sheila asked the cameraman suspiciously.

"No, it's perfect."

"Are you sure?"

"Absolutely."

"Good," Sheila nodded, accepting this. "How about you Steve, are you good?"

"I'm great!" said Steve enthusiastically. Bob shifted the camera angle to bring Walter's neighbour into frame. Much to Bob's surprise he now saw that Steve was wearing what appeared to be eyeliner and rouge. He tightened focus on the lens. It was definitely eyeliner and rouge badly applied and in bizarre contrast to the man's immaculate Armani suit. Steve's plastered on smile, which twitched noticeably at the corners, only served to heighten a sense of mania.

"Are you... wearing makeup?" asked Sheila tentatively.

Steve looked at her in surprise. "Of course. Aren't you?"

"Well, sure, but I'm a woman."

"Anchormen wear makeup."

"Yes, but that's done on set by professionals. It's meant to be very, you know, subtle."

"Are you saying this is too much?" asked Steve with concern.

"We're on in three," Bob interjected.

Sheila hesitated. There was no time to stop now. "No, it's fine. You look great. Perfect, in fact."

Steve nodded and smiled. The same easy confidence that allowed him to place multi-million dollar bets on Wall Street on a handshake and a rumour, allowed him to accept Sheila's assertion of his rightness with aplomb. It's a thin line, a professor at Harvard had once told him, between the extreme self-assurance needed to be a corporate CEO and megalomania, and the very best CEOs walk that line like a tightrope.

Bob counted down, "and... three... two... one."

Sheila's smile switched on like a light as she addressed the camera. "We're here again with Steve Prefect, immediate neighbour to Walter Parks." Steve nodded and smiled. "How are you managing, Steve, with a siege taking place literally in your own backyard?"

Steve's expression turned solemn. He wiped his eye, leaving a long streak of black mascara across his cheek. "Well, I won't lie to you, Sheila, it's been tough, really, really tough. But you know who I really, really, *really* worry about?"

"Who is that?"

"Dawn, Hope and yes, Walter Parks."

Sheila blinked. This was not the tirade she'd been expecting. "Really?"

Steve's face contorted into what he imagined sympathy must look like. "Sure, there are those who have been critical of Walter. Those who say he made his own mistakes, and now he needs to pay for them. They say 'life isn't fair' and 'that's how the ball bounces'. They say that, the reason I'm not in his shoes is because I'm somehow right and he's somehow wrong."

"Okay, but—"

"But I say to those people, aren't we all Walter Parks? Isn't America a nation of Walters? Walter is just a little man, struggling against the giant mechanics of these modern times. A man caught in the gears of a world grown so large that people's whole lives are just numbers on a spreadsheet to be bought and sold."

"Right, but–"

"Do you know Sheila, that the US Department of Health allows for sixteen insect parts per chocolate bar sold in this country? Plus one rodent hair."

"Um..."

"It's because a few bugs are considered simply the cost of doing business. I put it to you that we are all just bugs in the chocolate of modern society. Sure it's a chocolate that's rich, dark, and velvety smooth for those that get to eat it, but what about the bugs, I ask you, what about the bugs?"

Sheila stared at Steve, unsure what to make of this strange soliloquy. "So... Steve, this is quite a change of heart for you."

"I'm not sure what you mean."

"Well, this is our second interview and in our first interview you were quite critical of Walter."

Steve looked surprised and hurt. "That's your interpretation."

Sheila checked her notes. "You called him quote 'a bum' and told him to quote 'grow the hell up'."

"I believe you've taken that out of context," said Steve, "but perhaps I have softened my views somewhat."

"This change of heart wouldn't have anything to do with the fact that you work for Goldsmith-Price, a Securities Firm that has recently come into possession of Walter Parks's mortgage would it?"

Steve swallowed. He'd wanted to get out in front of that story, but he had not realized how close he'd cut it. It was he who'd requested the interview. This, however, explained why they'd so readily agreed to it. "No, not at all. I wasn't even aware of that fact," he said, feigning surprise.

Sheila thumbed through her notes once more, "Come to think of it, I believe Goldsmith-Price also owns shares in major chocolate companies and once lobbied to raise the number of acceptable bug parts to thirty, which would explain your knowledge on that particular subject."

"What you call 'bug parts' other cultures call protein, but regardless, is this really relevant to Walter Parks?"

"You're the one who brought it up, so—"

"Sometimes Sheila, it seems to me that the liberal media gets so caught up with trying to find a villain that they don't realize that maybe they should be looking in the mirror."

"What, are you..."

"Sometimes I feel like I'm the only one left watching out for poor Walter Parks."

"Really?"

"Really." Steve stared the woman reporter down with that same withering look he'd given those guys from the SEC as he informed them he'd had their car toed after first telling them they could park in his spot.

Sheila's response was not at all the same, however. She smiled with a disturbing glint in her eye. "Watching out for him like this, Mr. Prefect?"

Sheila nodded toward the camera and on queue the video feed switched to the recorded footage. She and Steve were able to watch it playback on a nearby monitor.

On the small screen was Steve from the day before, in his bathrobe, haranguing the Sheriff. The Sheriff, who seemed completely unmoved by the annoyed investment banker, popped the last piece of a doughnut into his mouth and reached for another. "...And what is it exactly you propose we do, Mr. Prefect?" asked the Sheriff.

"You have helicopters, just shoot him! Shoot Walter Parks in the head!"

The video froze on the last frame, zoomed in, Steve's beet-red face filled the screen. The vein on his temple looked particularly vibrant on the HD feed.

The real Steve stared in horror at his paused image, thus providing a perfect segue as the station cut back to live.

"I'm sorry, Mr. Prefect, did we take that out of context?" asked Sheila facetiously.

"Ahh!" shouted Steve in response. In that moment Steve saw his career shatter before his very eyes. In his mind, he saw a perfectly conceived crystal statue of himself being blown to smithereens in slow-motion by a high-speed golf ball. What followed was the snuffing out of any sense of reason or civilized self. A part of Steve's brain decided, at that moment, to chuck the last thirty-million years of evolution as a terrible mistake and revert to a non-lingual primitive state.

"I'm sorry?" asked Sheila.

"Ahhhhhhh. Ah!" said Steve. His face had begun to mirror the frozen image of itself.

"Mr. Prefect?"

Steve shoved Sheila aside and charged forward, crashing past Bob as well. Sheila cried out at the impact, while Bob adroitly pivoted to capture the now-deranged financier plowing through the crowd of surprised onlookers. "Ahhhhh!" Steve screamed.

"Uh, did you get that?" Sheila asked.

"Did I get it on camera? Yes. Did I understand it? No."

Steve had now disappeared into the crowd, but his position could still be easily determined by the path of upflung arms, thrown placards, and shouts as well as his own trailing cry of "Ahhhhhhh!"

CHAPTER 21

"...but, what if nobody came?" - Sun Tzu

Walter lunged forward, parrying the other swordsman's blow perfectly. His opponent loomed large above him—large and skewed slightly to the right. Walter raised his sword once more and his adversary, his own shadow on the living room wall, did the same, as always. Walter feigned a move to the left, then tilted his balance and, with a yell, stabbed boldly into the shadow's torso and deep into the drywall. The shadow had attempted a counterattack, but fell short, foiled again by the limits of its own two-dimensionality.

"Ah ha! And now for the coup de gras..." shouted Walter. He then attempted to retract the blade but found, to his surprise, that he could not. He yanked hard on the hilt, but somehow the sword tip had become firmly embedded inside the living room wall. Surprised, he gripped both quillons of the sword's crossguard and leaned back with first some, then all of his weight, to no avail. "Damn it," he cursed, "it's like it's stuck in stone." Walter planted one foot on the wall and, with grunts and groans, pulled until he fell onto his backside on the floor. The sword gave a *sproing!*—as it released from his grip, but remained none-the-less firmly implanted, vibrating. Walter shook his head in amazement and glanced about the room for some sort of tool he might use. As he did so, his eyes fell upon the television, still running on mute, in the corner. Much to Walter's surprise, Sancho was being interviewed. Walter crawled to within reach of the remote on the coffee table and pressed audio.

"...disappointed at the loss of your green card?" asked the CNN interviewer.

"Well, of course. I will no longer be able to send money to my family here in Mexico," said Sancho from what Walter now realized was a street in a Mexican village.

"And what about your role in the siege in New Jersey, any regrets there?" The interviewer tilted her microphone again towards Walter's friend.

"No, not at all. I would have stayed, but Walter made me go."

"He made you go... why?"

"Because he knew that if you lose this..." Sancho paused as he put his arm around his mother's shoulder, drawing her into frame. The small woman smiled broadly. The camera pulled back, bringing more of Sancho's family into view. "If you lose *this*, you lose *everything*."

Walter switched off the TV and tossed the remote to the floor. The plastic control spun to a stop at the corner of the sofa, knocking another, smaller object aside. Walter scurried over, awkwardly clattering in his suit of armour, to pick up a tiny figurine. "Sir Galahad!" he said as he recognized his lost knight, presumed eaten by Jesus weeks prior. He was still sad at the loss of King Arthur, but finding Galahad was somehow even better. For a moment, Walter admired the detail on the little lead figure. One tiny armoured hand clutched the now-missing sword. The other gauntlet seemed to be reaching for something unseen, something just out of reach. Walter knew what it was. Of all the knights of the round table, only Sir Galahad had been deemed worthy enough to lay eyes upon the Holy Grail. Not the great Lancelot, nor even Arthur himself. Only Galahad was *that good.* A moment of realization washed over Walter like a cold rain. He stuffed the knight into his belt pouch, scrambled to his feet and ran out into the hallway. "Dawn!" he shouted.

Walter paused a moment to listen for her response, but heard only silence. "Dawn?" He stomped up the stairs to the second floor—his armour plates rattling like dishes. "Dawn?" He stood on the second floor landing and waited for a response. Then, a movement outside the window caught his eye. It was Dawn on the front walk, moving with steady deliberation towards the front gate. Dawn held Hope in her arms and walked with a pace slowed by reluctance, but sustained by determination. Buffeted by the micro-hurricane created by a hovering news helicopter fifty feet above her head, she leaned forward to shelter the baby. On the neighbouring rooftops, sharpshooters focused their rifle sights. They were trained to do so on any potential target. The baby, after all, could be a bomb. From neighbouring windows, more news cameras tracked Dawn's every tenuous step. Jesus scampered along behind her, occasionally stopping to unleash a tirade of warning barks at the giant steel flying machine suspended in the air above. Jesus's barks were silent, swallowed by the helicopter's squall.

"Dawn?" Walter shouted pointlessly at the din. "Hope?"

*   *   *

Sheila stood in her familiar spot before the news camera with the siege playing out behind her. She was joined by actor Pierce Brosnan, who seemed as baffled as anyone by his presence there. On camera, the duo were reduced to a small picture-in-picture box in the lower left. It was the same setup the network used for commentary on the Macy's Day Parade. The rest of the screen showed the live aerial feed of Dawn's slow march down her own front walk.

"Thanks for joining us here Pierce," Sheila began, "for what now seems to be a pivotal moment in this standoff."

"My pleasure, Sheila." Pierce tried not to stare at the unsettling mess Sheila's hair had become. He began to worry that the localized weather systems generated by the several helicopters overhead might be the cause. He tried to catch a glimpse of his own hair in a nearby monitor to reassure himself. The bright glare of the sun on the screens, however, frustrated his efforts.

Sheila hesitated at the bizarre squinting and facial angling her guest was engaged in, before deciding it best not to ask. "It appears that, as we speak, Dawn Parks with her baby Hope in her arms, is walking towards the drawbridge. It may be that she is planning to give up to police. Is that what it looks like to you Pierce?"

"Absolutely," the actor replied. "I think we can all agree that she does appear to be walking towards the drawbridge, possibly to surrender."

"Definitely," nodded Sheila. "That definitely *appears* to be the case." On the news feed, Dawn, cradling Hope with great care, had now reached the closed drawbridge of the castle gate. "So is this how it's supposed to end, Pierce?"

"I think so, perhaps. It reminds me of the movie I'm starring in next November, called–"

At that moment, Pierce was interrupted by the sight of Walter bursting from the front door of the house, shouting and frantically waving his arms.

"Oh my," said Sheila. "Now it appears as if Walter Parks himself is charging after her."

"It does indeed, Sheila," the former James Bond star agreed ruefully, "it does indeed."

* * *

Dawn reached the front gate of the castle wall. The raised drawbridge blocking her way forward was built of thick boards of oak, reinforced with steel bands. A pair of garage-door openers jury-rigged on either side controlled the chains that could lower and raise the heavy slab. Dawn pressed the button, and the drawbridge began to descend, its chains cranking through the wall sockets. *Clack! Clack! Clack!* Dawn gently wiped some spittle from Hope's chin while they waited. With the roar of the helicopters and clamour of the crowd on the other side of the wall, she could not hear her husband yelling to her as he ran from the front door of the house. Dawn had made a clear decision not to look back.

Now as the drawbridge lowered into place across the moat, Dawn and the crowd, for the first time, came face to face. The onlookers and police were all mesmerized by the sight of this lone, wind-whipped woman holding a tiny child, framed by the castle gate.

"Dawn!" Walter cried. This time Dawn heard him. She turned to see the disheveled knight that was her husband, arrive panting behind her. His metal plates were askew and his left shoulder guard was lying on the lawn behind him, knocked off by the front door frame as he'd crashed through. He also had a terrible case of helmet-hair. "Dawn, honey, and Hope, I am so, so, sorry. I don't know what I was thinking, I..."

Dawn looked into his eyes and instantly knew all that he had to say. Walter wasn't trying to plead with her to stay. He was here to surrender. She didn't want that. Well, to the police, yes, but not to her. She only wanted him to be *with* herself and Hope. Dawn smiled, with that perfect charity that only she had. She loved Walter—that was never in question. She'd always loved him as he was, and felt it was high time that he did as well. Dawn opened her free arm, and Walter ran to her; hugging her as tightly as he could without hurting her. At the same time, Walter shook off his left gauntlet so he could safely touch Hope's cheek. The baby stirred from sleep and looked at Walter with half open eyes. A weak smile traced her tiny mouth. Dozens of video cameras and still-cameras captured every detail of the tender, intimate moment. News anchors everywhere said, "awww..."

In a cocktail lounge in Munich, Wilhelm Schmidt watched the scene on a television hanging in the corner. He shook his head at the crazy American movie, and reached for another handful of cocktail peanuts. Across the bar from him sat two unemployed factory workers from what had formerly been East Germany. They sipped waters and waited. They planned to jump him in the alley once he left the bar for whatever was in his wallet.

"Can you possibly forgive me?" Walter begged his wife.

"Of course!" She then smiled and said, "After all, what would Jesus do?" Jesus barked at the sound of his name. Dawn looked down at the dog wagging his tail by her side. "Either one," she added, giving Jesus a pat. Walter relaxed visibly. "Can we go now?" she asked.

Walter nodded and smiled. He took her hand and all three walked bravely towards the phalanx of police and media that lay on the other side of the drawbridge.

The sharpshooter on the roof of Steve Prefect's house watched the scene play out through the sight of his rifle. He would continue to follow Walter in this way until the suspect was patted down and handcuffed in custody. The sharpshooter was watching for any sudden movement or hint of a bomb. The sharpshooter's finger rested on the trigger of his gun, relaxed but ready. His experience told him that this was over, but his training told him to follow it through. What he wasn't aware of was Steve Prefect standing on the roof behind him. Steve wasn't supposed to be there.

Steve Prefect was, in simple terms, no longer completely sane. The vein on his forehead was now permanently engorged, one of his eyes bulged in an allergic reaction to the mascara he'd put on earlier, and he twitched involuntarily, as if somewhere in his brain a pair of vengeful lab rats were applying a mild electric shock. The sharpshooter continued to remain unaware of Steve. Both men completely focused their attention on Walter and Dawn below.

"Oh wait, I forgot something," said Walter, stopping in his tracks midway across the drawbridge.

Television audiences around the world held their collective breath. Commentators in Brazil reported Walter's hesitation as if it were a surprise move at the World Cup. "What's this?" they shouted.

"What?" asked Dawn.

"Just a minute. I'll be back in a minute, I promise!" Walter gave a last, affirming half smile that he hoped conveyed that he wasn't being crazy, and headed back towards the house. Jesus turned and followed fast on his master's heels.

"Walter, what could be so important?" Dawn called after him, to no avail.

* * *

Steve stared in disbelief as Walter crossed back over the drawbridge and through the castle gate. He had been anxiously anticipating the glorious moment of Walter's arrest. In his mind's eye Walter would, despite walking out voluntarily, then resist arrest and be tased and viciously beaten into submission. The judge would reinstitute public stocks as a legal form of punishment. Steve, in turn, would then spend his time hurling dog poop and yelling obscenities at Walter. In his mind, it was a beautiful sight. Now, however, this one modest dream seemed to be slipping away, and it simply wasn't fair. "No, no, no!" Steve cried in despair.

The sharpshooter lying prone on the roof's edge looked up from his rifle-sight in surprise. "Sir, you're not supposed to be up here."

"This is my roof," Steve pointed out.

"Oh. Well, regardless sir, you're still–"

"Look! Look at him! You're letting him get away! You can't let him get away. He ruined my life!"

The sharpshooter tried to gauge the crazed look in Steve's eyes. The man's flailing arms and apparent transvestite makeover made the policeman wonder if he might be the more immediate threat. "Sir," he ordered, "get down off this roof, immediately."

Steve fumed, and clenched his fists in anger, but then turned, as if to leave. His orders being what they were, the marksman put his eye back to the rifle-sight. He smoothly tilted the telescopic lens to bring Walter once more into view. Walter, having tripped over his own scabbard, landing facedown in Dawn's marigolds, had failed yet to reach the front door. The errant-knight was on his feet again, however, and now almost there.

"No!" yelled Steve. Suddenly, the sharpshooter felt the full weight of a six-foot-two inch Wall Street investment banker landing on his back. The wind knocked out of him, the officer was only barely able to keep Steve from wrestling the gun from his grip.

"Let go!" demanded Steve.

"What the hell?" cried the astonished officer.

"Shoot him! We need to shoot him!"

The two men rolled back and forth on the roof's edge, unseen by the crowd below who were transfixed by Walter. Their hero currently trying to untangle his front door keys from his own codpiece.

"Ahhh!" yelled Steve reverting to the primal ranting that he felt best expressed his current state of mind. They wrestled on the precipice as, below, Walter finally unlocked and opened the door to his house. At that moment, Steve suddenly stopped trying to steal the rifle and instead slid down his hand over the sharpshooter's and squeezed. The marksman, whose finger was still inside the trigger guard, was forced to fire.

The bullet exploded from the precision crafted barrel. Despite their rooftop wrestling and high angle-to-distance odds, the bullet miraculously fired on a direct trajectory to Walter's head. It would have been, under normal circumstances, a kill-shot. Normal circumstances, of course, would have included a target who wasn't wearing a solid steel recreation of a twelfth-century knight's helmet. That not being the case, however, the bullet instead ricocheted off of the side of Walter's head with a loud *ding!* The impact left a deep dent in the metal and sent Walter reeling, but still very much alive. Not content with this, the bullet continued on its way, at a ninety-degree angle, through the front door of the house. It proceeded there directly to the kitchen where it found itself on a collision course with the kettle on the stove. Again, the now somewhat slowed munition struck steel, sending the kettle flying and itself in an entirely new direction. This time it met with the kitchen wall which, built from cheap and ultimately toxic Chinese drywall, proved far less resistant than the previous metal surfaces. It therefore passed through the wall and outside once more. There it found its final resting place, one of the rows of gasoline barrels lined up along the side of the house. The bullet grazed the side of a barrel, severing the casing and creating a teeny, tiny spark...

Walter, stunned by the powerful impact on the side of his head, staggered blindly into the living room of his home. He was unsure what had caused the sharp impact on his helmet, but his battered brain was currently floating the theory that invisible golf playing gods were practicing putts with his cranium. He had other theories but, thus far, he felt this was the most plausible. For a moment, he had a strange vision of his head rolling towards spinning windmill blades. That vision was then obliterated by the sudden explosion of six barrels of gasoline at the side of the house. *Ka-Boom!*

* * *

Dawn watched in disbelief as a massive fireball engulfed the house. She crumpled to the earth in horror, instinctively shielding Hope from the catastrophic conflagration. "No! Walter!" she cried out, starting forward even as a wall of super-heated air buffeted her back. Two police officers grabbed her arms and pulled her away, easily overpowering her efforts. "We need to save Walter," she begged. She was confused by their seeming lack of comprehension. "We need to save him!"

A short distance away, Sheila, along with the rest of the onlookers, stared dumbstruck at the sudden inferno the castle had become. Bob, the cameraman, witnessed it as always through the protective glass of the camera viewfinder. He sniffed the smokey air and thought to himself, is this what an Emmy smells like? Do Emmys smell like burning human flesh? Bob, who had never actually smelt burning human flesh before, then thought, "burning human flesh smells a lot like bacon." He then felt somewhat disturbed by his next thought, since Bob was a big fan of bacon. Of course, what Bob was smelling actually was bacon. The kitchen, being adjacent to the barrels of gasoline, was the first to go and Walter, also a big fan of bacon, had stocked the refrigerator with several pounds of it to last out the siege.

The Siege of Walter Parks

Steve Prefect chuckled with glee and danced his way through the appalled crowd. For a moment he'd thought his efforts to bring justice to the world had been thwarted, but the explosion and fire were far more than he could ever have hoped for. He then heard a sound above the roar of the flames, a sound that made his heart sink. It was the sound of sirens. The crowd were awoken from their horrorstruck trance by the massive bulk of an arriving firetruck. The people parted to allow the big red vehicle through. Firemen jumped down to the street in front of the castle. They dragged hoses behind them, clearing paths to the only available fire hydrant, on the other side of the road. In moments, they had two hoses attached, each turgid with water pressure. They then dragged them over the drawbridge and into the ward of the castle. "You can't let him die... you can't let him!" Dawn pleaded with them desperately, still clutching Hope close to her bosom. The firemen aimed the nozzles at the flames and turned the small control valves, releasing a blast of water high into the air and down onto the burning house. The castle walls, designed by Walter to protect the home, now stopped the crews from reaching the home from the adjacent lots or the street behind. For now, until air support could arrive, the frontal approach was the only one available to the firefighters. Still, the twin fountains of water began to have a visible effect on the flames.

Forgotten in the chaos, Steve crept unseen around to the back of the firetruck. The view of the spectacle was obstructed here by the massive vehicle, so the street was open and empty of onlookers. Steve snatched a fire axe from the side of the truck and approached the first of the two hoses. With a "Hee-hee!" of pure glee, he lifted the axe high above his head and swung down. The blade easily chopped through the taut canvas tube. A geyser of released water blasted upwards into Steve's face, sending him flying to the ground, sputtering and spitting.

Back in the castle ward one of the fireman stared in astonishment as the flow of water vanished and the hose in his hand fell limp.

Steve pulled himself up against the firetruck and wiped the water from his eyes. The hydraulic blast had waterlogged every orifice in his face, leaving his nose running like that of an unattended toddler. He shook his head sideways in an attempt to clear what felt like a small ocean between his ears.

"Hey, he's cutting the hoses!" someone shouted.

The crowd turned to see who the villain might be. With nowhere to hide, Steve boldly stood and sneered at them. Petty humans, he thought, I am Megwah. Like an ancient God, he faced them down with a look of utter contempt, brandishing the bright-red fire axe. Time to cut the grass, he thought.

"He's got an axe!" shouted somebody with a talent for stating the obvious.

Steve, who could no longer hear properly because of the aforementioned water in his ears, shouted back defiantly, "No, I won't pay more tax!"

There was a confusing moment as the crowd considered the correct response to this complete non sequitur. Most of them didn't want to pay more taxes either.

Steve broke the impasse by lifting the axe and running to the second, still functioning, fire hose. "Back! Stand back!" he cried. With a mighty chop, he severed the second canvas tube, this time carefully sidestepping the fountain blast from the hole. He looked in delight at his handiwork before taunting the crowd. "So, who's the loser now?" he laughed. With this, he tripped backwards over the first hose and landed, once more, on his backside.

At that moment the last barrel of gasoline at the side of Walter's house exploded. Positioned under the American Dream billboard which had once adorned Walter's front lawn, the explosion sent said billboard flipping fifty feet up into the air. For a moment, the burning sign hung at the apex of its flight as if deciding what to do. The sign then fell, having apparently chosen to make its last moment as ironic as possible, and plunged with a crash through Steve's roof. Instantly, the flames from the sign transferred to the shingles and exposed framework, swiftly setting Steve Prefect's entire house on fire.

"God damn it!" shouted Steve, throwing the axe to the ground. Seeing their opportunity, the crowd rushed him, piling on and burying him with their bodies.

* * *

The firemen, bereft of their best weapons against the roaring flames, could only watch the two houses burn and call for backup.

"Why don't you save him? Why?" Dawn sobbed.

"I'm sorry ma'am. It's simply too dangerous."

Dawn stared at the firefighter. His somber expression spoke the truth, and the inferno that had once been their home confirmed it. Still, Dawn had always believed in miracles, and miracles, by definition, defied apparent truth.

The other firefighter nodded his agreement, "It's out of our hands."

CHAPTER 22

"At least it's a dry heat." - J. d'Arc

The inside of the Parks's family home was roughly the same temperature as a microwave burrito when it's just been taken out of the microwave. That's the time when the only way to hold it is to pass it rapidly back and fourth between your fingers and biting into it can lead to serious tongue damage. Of course, the parts of the home that were actually on fire were even hotter than this, while other currently less combustive parts were more like Palm Springs in the summer. Still, overall, the average was just about burrito.

Walter and Dawn's bedroom was one of the hotter areas in the home. The bed itself was in flames that licked the ceiling. The curtains burned and fell. The knights on Walter's dresser sank into multicoloured pools of molten lead. Sir Gawain flowed fictitiously into William the Conqueror who in turn merged into an anachronistic sludge with Sir Mowbray.

In the living room, the television continued to play even as part of the ceiling collapsed and burning timbers fell to the carpet. Sheila Blitz, half-obscured by a smudge of soot, continued her coverage. "...what has turned out to be a sad ending for Walter Parks." The TV itself caught fire at that moment, but continued to function even as the casing burned. "Whether you consider him folk hero or deadbeat, no one wanted this sort of ending for–" Suddenly the heat cracked the screen and the signal died, leaving the room filled with the sound of roaring flames.

A few feet away, Walter groaned and lifted his head. His armoured form was covered in refrigerator magnets that had somehow been blown out of the kitchen and attached themselves to him. He pushed away a plastic pineapple magnet from his nose. Now awake, he became instantly aware of the sudden resemblance that his house had to the inside of a pizza oven. "The living room isn't normally engulfed in flames..." his badly abused brain observed. He tried to lift his body but found his efforts blocked. A heavy wooden ceiling beam, which really by definition ought to be in the ceiling, was now inexplicably laying across his backside. "Well, that doesn't seem right either" thought his brain. His brain then made a rather unimpressive cognitive leap, "My house is on fire." Next his brain thought, "And I'm inside it." His brain then made another cognitive shuffle forward, "I'm going to die." His brain then immediately wished it had not made this last leap and tried to jump back only to discover it could not, as the way back was now on fire. At that moment the television flickered once more to life, showing a camera zoom in on Dawn, still clutching Hope, but on her knees before the burning house. Tears ran down Dawn's cheek. "They're safe," thought Walter. "At least, they're safe."

The audio cut in for a moment with Sheila reporting in voiceover, "...where Dawn Parks refuses to leave."

"Dawn," Walter said, even though he knew it wasn't one of those two-way televisions that hadn't been invented yet. "Dawn... I'm so..." The television died once more, this time for real.

Walter tried to lift himself up again, with all of his strength. In his effort, he gasped too much smoke and too little oxygen and began to cough ferociously. His head reeled, and he sank unconscious to the floor once more.

A burning chunk of ceiling crashed next to Walter's face and began the slow process of barbecuing him. He had already acquired a smokey flavour. Before he was even medium rare; however, Walter's face began to move. It moved in a slow slide across the floor, a few inches before stopping. It then moved again, a few more inches. Move, stop, move, stop. In fits and starts, Walter was being dragged out from under the fallen beam and towards the front door of the house. Move, stop. Jesus panted hoarsely for a moment. There was no time to think, which suited Jesus just fine. The dog gripped Walter's pant leg again between his teeth and tugged. Move, stop.

*   *   *

The paramedics gently, but firmly pulled Dawn away from the collapsing structure that had once been her home. The sound of wailing sirens foretold the arrival of more fire trucks with more hoses, but the damage was done. They would arrive to stop the fire from spreading and to make the area safe, but both houses were far beyond saving.

"I'm sorry ma'am. It's time to go," insisted the paramedic kindly, but firmly. She wanted to pry the baby from Dawn's arms, but any attempt to do so proved impossible.

"No," said Dawn.

"It's time to give up."

"No... no."

"What the hell?" said one of the fireman as he peered incredulously into the smoke-filled front door of the home. "Is that a dog?"

As they watched, the grey silhouette of a dog's hindquarters materialized out of the haze.

"It is a dog!"

"Jesus!" shouted Dawn.

"Jesus Christ!" agreed the fireman.

Jesus inched his way out of the smoke until the reason for his ass-backwards progression became apparent.

"He's got Walter!" Dawn whispered, then shouted, "He's got Walter!"

The two firemen rushed forward to lift the unconscious knight from the front door after only the second bounce of his head on the front step. A third fireman lifted the smoke-addled dog to his shoulder and carried him to safety. Jesus weakly licked the stranger's cheek before sinking into his arms.

Dawn ran to meet her husband. His clothes and hair were singed, and his skin was coated in soot. His legs, however, moved in an unconscious ghost dance, as if trying to walk, proving that he still lived.

In his arms, Walter clutched something. Despite its being charred from the fire, Dawn recognized it immediately as Hope's Baby Book. What a fool, she thought, what a wonderful fool.

CHAPTER 23

"We're gonna need a bigger needle." - J. Osteen

"Take your stinking paws off me, you damned dirty ape!" Steve snarled at the police officer who led him away in handcuffs.

Sheila moved quickly to intercept Walter's deranged neighbour. "Mr. Prefect, why did you do this?" she shouted and extended her microphone to catch his response.

"Me? This is all your fault," he said, as if pointing out the obvious.

Sheila stopped in surprise. This was not one of the answers she'd expected. Based on her past interactions with Steve, she'd anticipated him blaming Walter, declaring himself the victim, or carrying on in a prelingual primal display. Blaming her, however, was not on her list of expected responses. "What? Why?" she asked him.

Steve began giggling stupidly as if he'd told her a joke of which she was the butt and too dense to know it. The police officer pushed Steve's head down as he forced him into the back of the police cruiser and shut the door. Sheila could hear Steve's maniacal chuckles continue from inside as they drove away.

* * *

Walter lay flat on the gurney; sucking in the sweet tasting oxygen from the mask the paramedic had placed over his nose and mouth. He was in a smoke induced stupor and viewed the blue sky and occasional passing person with half lidded eyes. Then, someone else appeared against the blue. He squinted to see the face, but he already knew who they were. He pushed aside the mask and gasped, "Dawn... Hope?"

"We're both here," smiled Dawn. She crouched down and lifted Hope for Walter to see. His daughter smiled faintly at the sight of her father and blew small bubbles of spit.

"Is she all right?"

"Yes, we're all fine." Dawn glanced at the Sheriff who stood a short distance away, supervising them with stern disapproval. "You may be away from us for a while, but we're all going to be okay."

"We can finish Hope's book?"

Dawn nodded and put her hand on the baby book Walter still clutched. Efforts to remove the book from his grasp had been in vain. Especially after Dawn had vetoed the Sheriff's suggestion of needle-nose pliers.

"What happened?"

"Don't you know?" smiled Dawn. "Jesus saved you, of course."

"Jesus?" Jesus appeared at the sound of his name and began licking Walter's sooty cheeks enthusiastically. "Oh, who's a good boy?" asked Walter. "Yes, you are! Yes, you are..." Jesus wagged his tail and began to lick the inside of Walter's ear. Walter closed his eyes, blindly reached and found Dawn's hand and squeezed it tight.

And so it was. Dawn, of course, praised the Almighty and said how it all confirmed her faith. She said that the Lord loved them so much he had sent his only dog. Sancho felt they'd struck a blow for the common man and later landed a role as a celebrity soccer commentator in Mexico. Others felt Walter got what he deserved. What did it all mean? Likely nothing. After all, in the end, Walter still lost his home and, for a while, his freedom. The bank collected the insurance. The news media moved on. The global economy collapsed sometime later, and soon it seemed everyone was losing their homes. Steve went to jail, but his bosses all got even richer when Goldsmith-Price was bought up by one of the big banks as part of a government bailout. Maybe it all happened for a reason, but most likely not. What really mattered was that, in the end, in their little tiny corner of existence, Walter still had Dawn and, together, they still had Hope. Oh and yes, Walter was permitted to personally stick Hope's first birthday photo, taken on family visiting day in prison, into her baby book.

The End

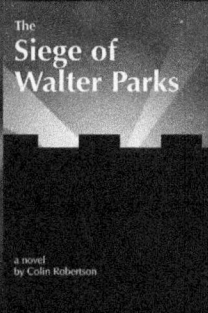

About the Author

Colin Robertson was originally from Toronto, Canada. Determined not to be ruined by success, he decided to become an indie author in 2012 with the publication of his debut novel, *The Siege of Walter Parks*. He completed his second novel *Chaos Theory* in 2015 (Winner: Forward Indie Bronze Medal for Science Fiction), and his third novel *Spyware* in 2018. He is the author of several short stories and optioned screenplays and currently lives with his wife, son, daughter and very loud wheaten terrier in Culver City, California.

www.ingramcontent.com/pod-product-compliance
Lightning Source LLC
Chambersburg PA
CBHW051822040426
42447CB00006B/330